THE RIGHT OF THE PEOPLE

BOOKS BY WILLIAM O. DOUGLAS

THE RIGHT OF THE PEOPLE

RUSSIAN JOURNEY

WE THE JUDGES

AN ALMANAC OF LIBERTY

NORTH FROM MALAYA

BEYOND THE HIGH HIMALAYAS

STRANGE LANDS AND FRIENDLY PEOPLE

OF MEN AND MOUNTAINS

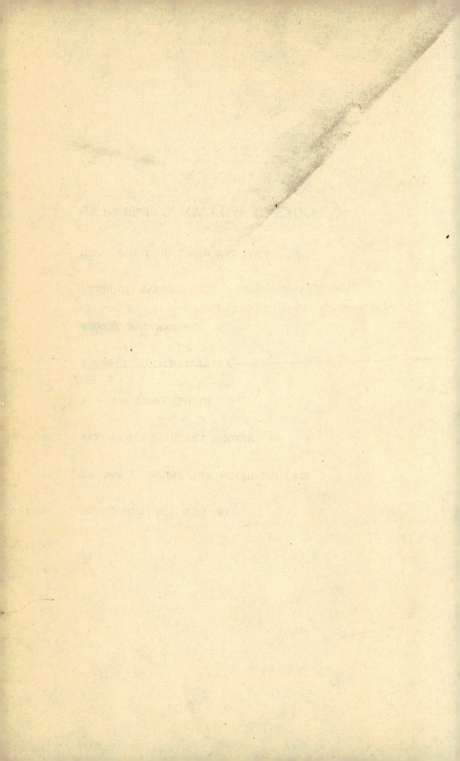

This book is in substantial part the North Lectures delivered at Franklin and Marshall College in the spring of 1957.

The Right of the People

of the

People

BY WILLIAM O. DOUGLAS

1958

DOUBLEDAY & COMPANY, INC., GARDEN CITY, NEW YORK

Library of Congress Catalog Card Number 58–5571
Copyright © 1958 by William O. Douglas
All Rights Reserved. Printed in the United States of America
Designed by Alma Reese Cardi

FOREWORD

This is the time for us to become the champions of the virtues that have given the West great civilizations. These virtues are reflected in our attitudes and ways of thought, not in our standard of living. They are found in the ideas of justice, liberty, and equality that are written into the American Constitution. They concern the rights of the people against the state. These rights include the right to speak and write as one chooses, the right to follow the dictates of one's conscience, the right to worship as one desires. They include the right to be let alone in a myriad of ways, including the right to defy government at times and tell it not to intermeddle. These rights of the people also include the right to manage the affairs of the nation—civil and military—and to be free of military domination or direction.

These are the rights that distinguish us from all totalitarian regimes. The real enemies of freedom are not confined to any nation or any country. They are everywhere. They flourish where injustice, discrimination, ignorance, superstition, intolerance, and arbitrary power exist. We cannot afford to inveigh against them abroad, unless we are alert to guard against them at home. Yet in recent years as we have denounced the loss of liberty abroad we have witnessed its decline here. We have, indeed, been retreating from our democratic ideals at home. We have compromised them for security reasons.

It is time to put an end to the retreat. It is time we made these virtues truly positive influences in our policies. We have a moral authority in our ideals of justice, liberty, and equality that is indestructible. If we live by those virtues, we will rejuvenate America. If we make them our offensive at home and abroad, we will quicken the hearts of men the world around. The contest is on for the uncommitted people of the earth. These ideals express the one true advantage we have over communism in that contest.

WILLIAM O. DOUGLAS

CONTENTS

CONTENTS

LECTURE III: THE CIVILIAN AUTHORITY

Freedom of Expression

I. THE PHILOSOPHY
OF THE FIRST AMENDMENT

When Khrushchev and Bulganin were visiting England, they met with Hugh Gaitskell and other Labor Party members. The meeting led to an acrimonious exchange of words, Khrushchev challenging Gaitskell to tell him the difference between "your democracy and ours." Gaitskell replied in a flash, "Read Pericles' funeral oration."

Pericles talked about the secret of happiness: courage, he said, was freedom and freedom was happiness; and freedom was available only to those with brave hearts. Discussion and debate are often finer badges of bravery than battle itself. Pericles said, "The great impediment to action is, in our opinion, not discussion, but the want of that knowledge which is gained by discussion preparatory to action. For we have a peculiar power of thinking before we act, and of acting too; whereas other men are courageous from ignorance but hesitate upon reflection."

In the totalitarian state there is freedom of expression in a limited sense. In Russia there are great debates concerning the course to follow, the choice of procedures, the policy that should be adopted in factories or on farms. Criticism fills the papers and magazines of Russia. But this criticism and debate do not challenge communism as a system. Rather, they assume that communism is the ideal state. Once that postulate is express or implied, discussion and debate go on apace. The same seems to be true in Red China, where the communist regime recently approved a new slogan derived from the Chinese classics: "Let hundreds of schools crow in competition." Yet in both Soviet Russia and Red China, if the discussion goes so far as to question the premise on which communism rests, it is condemned as counterrevolutionary.

My thesis is that there is no free speech in the full meaning of the term unless there is freedom to challenge the very postulates on which the existing regime rests. It is my belief that our First Amendment must be placed in that broad frame of reference and construed to permit even discourse or advocacy that strikes at the very foundation of our institutions. The First Amendment was a new and bold experiment. It staked everything on unlimited public discussion. It chose among conflicting values, selecting the freedom to talk, to argue, and to advocate as a preferred right. It placed us on the side of free discussion and advocacy, come what may.

None of the state constitutions prior to 1787 (save the much debated Pennsylvania Constitution of 1776) contained any mention of freedom of speech; and only seven of the thirteen States wrote into their constitutions any guarantee of freedom of the press. Moreover, in those days freedom of the press meant something far less than it does today. In the beginning it meant only freedom from prior restraint. An author or publisher could be held accountable for publishing what the regime thought was against "the public good." The First Amendment did not build on existing law; it broke with tradition, set a new standard, and exalted freedom of expression.

Hamilton had argued against the need for a Bill of Rights. He maintained that freedom of the press, for example, "must altogether depend on public opinion; and on the general spirit of the people and of the government," particularly on "legislative discretion." *The Federalist*, No. 84. There were those who did not trust the people, who felt that government need keep a firm hand on the citizen if the nation was to survive.

Jefferson, the spiritual father of the Bill of Rights, and Madison, the astute politician who steered the Bill of Rights through Congress, were of a different school of thought. They recognized the risk of tyranny of the majority. But they had confidence in popular rule and confidence in a Bill of Rights as a restraint on "the tyranny of the legislatures" and as an aid to the judiciary in preventing encroachments on the liberty of the citizen.

Moreover, both Jefferson and Madison were convinced that the only wise policy was to keep the market place of ideas unregulated by the government. Madison wrote:

"A popular Government, without popular information, or the means of acquiring it, is but a Prologue to a Farce or a Tragedy; or, perhaps both. Knowledge will forever govern ignorance: And a people who mean to be their

19

own Governors, must arm themselves with the power which knowledge gives."

Jefferson stoutly maintained over the years that "Truth is the proper and sufficient antagonist to error." On January 16, 1787, he wrote:

"I am persuaded myself that the good sense of the people will always be found to be the best army. They may be led astray for a moment, but will soon correct themselves. The people are the only censors of their governors; and even their errors will tend to keep them to the true principles of their institution. To punish these errors too severely would be to suppress the only safeguard of the public liberty. The way to prevent these irregular interpositions of the people, is to give them full information of their affairs through the channel of the public papers, and to contrive that those papers should penetrate the whole mass of the people. The basis of our governments being the opinion of the people, the very first object should be to keep that right; and were it left to me to decide whether we should have a government without newspapers, or newspapers without a government, I should not hesitate a moment to prefer the latter."

The extent to which Jefferson would go in sustaining freedom of speech was indicated in his First Inaugural. At that time the country boiled under the heat generated by the obnoxious Alien and Sedition Laws of 1798. Tempers were high; terror was loose in some communities;

the nation was fast becoming a divided house. Yet Jefferson said, "If there be any among us who would wish to dissolve this Union or to change its republican form, let them stand undisturbed as monuments of the safety with which error of opinion may be tolerated where reason is left free to combat it."

The First Amendment does not say that there is freedom of expression provided the talk is not "dangerous." It does not say that there is freedom of expression provided the utterance has no tendency to subvert. It does not put free speech and freedom of the press in the category of housing, sanitation, hours of work, factory conditions, and the like, and make it subject to regulation for the public good. Nor does it permit legislative restraint of freedom of expression so long as the regulation does not offend due process. All notions of regulation or restraint by government are absent from the First Amendment. For it says in words that are unambiguous, "Congress shall make no law . . . abridging the freedom of speech, or of the press. . . ."

This guarantee plays a unique role. The compact of the Constitution is a compact of We The People. The ultimate political power is in the people. They can alter, revise, or undo what they created any time they choose. While the compact lasts, the various agencies of government are responsible to the people. The people elect their law-makers and their Chief Executive for limited terms only. Those who exercise authority must have it recurringly renewed at the hands of the people. The people are, indeed, the final repository of all power. This political truth was first clearly stated on these shores by George Mason in the Virginia

Declaration of Rights, adopted June 12, 1776: "That all power is vested in, and consequently derived from, the people; that magistrates are their trustees and servants, and at all times amenable to them."

The emergence on this continent of that concept of sovereignty had a special history. It was revolutionary because it struck at the *status quo*. It remains today a revolutionary concept in most areas of the world, parts of Europe and the Americas not excepted.

So long as the sovereign power was in the hands of an hereditary, mercantile, financial, or landowner group, there never was, nor is today, any freedom of expression. When a select group is in power, it demands respect and obedience.

Every majority tends to acquire a vested interest in the *status quo*. The values represented by their economic, political, racial, or religious interests seem to them to be the expression of the ultimate. They cling tenaciously to them and look on the minority with antagonism and suspicion. In a state under the domination of the church, the teaching of evolution might be deemed subversive. In a state ruled by atheists, religion might be a dangerous subject.

As May wrote in the *Constitutional History of England*, "Everywhere authority has resented discussion, as hostile to its own sovereign rights." A monarchy, oligarchy, or other dictatorship keeps a tight rein on discussion and on the press. Under those conditions there is no real freedom, as we know it, unless the discussion accepts the premise on which the existing regime rests. Madison maintained that freedom of the press saved the States from being "miserable colonies" suffering under a foreign yoke. Certainly the value of freedom of expression grew in the minds of Americans as the struggle for independence went on. But the people did not fully acquire that right until they acquired complete sovereignty. It is not surprising then to find freedom of expression emerging on this continent as a political right only as the independence movement got under full swing in the latter quarter of the eighteenth century. It is, I think, true that freedom of expression is one of the last political rights which any people acquire.

When sovereignty rests in a man or in a majority, suppression of a minority may be necessary to protect and safeguard the *status quo*. But when sovereignty is in the people, it is distributed equally and indivisibly among every member of the group. The conformists and the non-conformists alike can claim the privilege. So can the reactionaries and the revolutionaries, those who believe in *laissez faire* and those who believe in the dictatorship of the proletariat. That, at least, is the theory. And freedom of expression is as integral a part of the rights of sovereignty as running for office or voting.

Freedom of expression is a necessary political right once the people have the full right of sovereignty. It is indeed the only guarantee that the people will be kept adequately informed to discharge the awesome responsibilities of sovereignty. Without freedom of expression, only some public issues might be canvassed. Without it, the nation might drift to a pattern of conformity that loses all relation to the world and its large affairs.

Erskine said that liberty of opinion keeps governments

themselves in due subjection to their duties. But it strikes deeper than that. It assures the opportunity to reform. Change is the law of politics, if there is to be survival. As Burke said, "A state without the means of some change is without the means of its conservation." Freedom of expression and the right to resort to the polls are the only instruments available to minorities to wage political and educational campaigns against the *status quo* of their day.

This right, if it is to be a vital one, must extend to the lowliest, the smallest, the most despised minority of all. John Stuart Mill stated the reason in words that have become classic:

"If all mankind minus one were of one opinion, and only one person were of the contrary opinion, mankind would be no more justified in silencing that one person, than he, if he had the power, would be justified in silencing mankind. Were an opinion a personal possession of no value except to the owner; if to be obstructed in the enjoyment of it were simply a private injury, it would make some difference whether the injury was inflicted only on a few persons or on many. But the peculiar evil of silencing the expression of an opinion is, that it is robbing the human race; posterity as well as the existing generation; those who dissent from the opinion, still more than those who hold it. If the opinion is right, they are deprived of the opportunity of exchanging error for truth: if wrong, they lose, what is almost as great a benefit, the clearer perception and livelier impression of truth, produced by its collision with error."

24

Freedom of expression must cover the entire public domain. The public domain includes more than election issues. This was early recognized in the struggle for liberty which went on in this country in the eighteenth century. The Continental Congress, moved by strong currents of independence, communicated in 1774 with the settlers in Canada, seeking their cooperation. While the *Quebec Letter* spoke of freedom of the press as an ally of political rights, it did not so restrict it:

"The last right we shall mention, regards the freedom of the press. The importance of this consists, besides the advancement of truth, science, morality, and arts in general, in its diffusion of liberal sentiments on the administration of Government, its ready communication of thoughts between subjects, and its consequential promotion of union among them, whereby oppressive officers are shamed or intimidated, into more honourable and just modes of conducting affairs."

If the people are to be wise sovereigns, there must be no restraints or limits on cultural, scientific, artistic, or intellectual endeavor.

Under our system of government, strictly private groups may commit themselves to the propagation of one point of view or philosophy if they so desire. But public agencies by force of the First Amendment, which is made applicable to the States by the Due Process Clause of the Fourteenth Amendment, are barred from putting the quietus on any school of thought. Government may not deprive the citizen of any branch of learning nor bar any avenue of research

25

nor ban any type of discourse. The prohibition extends to private discourse between citizens, public discourse through any channel of communication, or teaching in any classroom.

Every generation, if it is to grow to maturity and have understanding of man and the universe, must have no limits to its horizons. In Plato's *Republic* the state would dominate and control education, dictating how literature, poetry, art, music, and even gymnastics are to be taught. In our society the search for knowledge must be free and unhampered. The spirit of free inquiry must be allowed to dominate the schools and universities. "Universities should not be transformed, as in Nazi Germany, into loudspeakers for men who wield political power." Chafee, *The Blessings of Liberty* (1956), p. 241. Teachers must be allowed to pursue ideas into any domain. There must be no terminal points on discourse. The classical statement of that position was made by Robert M. Hutchins:

"Education is a kind of continuing dialogue, and a dialogue assumes, in the nature of the case, different points of view.

"The civilizations which I work and which I am sure every American is working toward, could be called a civilization of the dialogue, where instead of shooting one another when you differ, you reason things out together.

"In this dialogue, then, you cannot assume that you are going to have everybody thinking the same way or feeling the same way. It would be unprogressive if that happened. The hope of eventual development would be gone. More than that, of course, it would be very boring.

"A university, then, is a kind of continuing Socratic conversation on the highest level for the very best people you can think of, you can bring together, about the most important questions, and the thing that you must do to the uttermost possible limits is to guarantee those men the freedom to think and to express themselves.

"Now, the limits on this freedom cannot be merely prejudice, because although our prejudices might be perfectly satisfactory, the prejudices of our successors or of those who are in a position to bring pressure to bear on the institution, might be subversive in the real sense, subverting the American doctrine of free thought and free speech."

Public opinion—the basis on which our society rests—must be responsible and responsive. To be such it must be disciplined and informed. It cannot be disciplined and informed unless those who shape it have the opportunities for critical inquiry, for the cultivation of open-mindedness, for the search for truth in every recess of the universe. This freedom of inquiry must be allowed to embrace all realms of knowledge—the arts as well as religion and science. An appreciation of the arts is often necessary for intelligent law making. The legislative function aside, an appreciation of the arts helps produce a society that is civilized, cultured, and mature by allowing individuals to cultivate their utmost capacities.

Literature has been a classic form for the dissemination

of ideas. When an author describes in minute detail a way of life, the description itself may be mute criticism of that way of life or the conditions which bring it about. ". . . this entrance into lives wider and more various than our own in turn enables us more nicely to appreciate and more intensely to live the lives we do know." Edman, *Arts and the Man* (1939), p. 84.

Advocates of the abolition of slavery, of economic and social reform, of the pure food and drug laws, have found allies in the authors of fiction. Dissatisfaction with existing social, economic, political, and moral conditions can normally be more eloquently expressed in a novel than in a scholarly polemic. That is one reason why government control over literary standards is so repugnant to Americans. Under government censorship and control, literature can be reduced to pallid and inoffensive discourses on the *status quo*.

What is trash or trivia to one may be precious to others. The tastes of men differ widely. So does the impact of ideas. Lurid sex accounts may trigger a seriously ill psychopath into some kind of action; and yet in another person add to the sober knowledge of life and help avoid the development of neurotic tendencies. The demands of freedom of expression require government to keep its hands off all literature. Literature performs the important social function of exposing all facets of life. It loses an important social function when it is subjected to the demands of the prevailing morality. Literature and morality should enjoy competitive co-existence. Literature is the vehicle of ideas, of knowledge—unrestricted by the political, religious, or moral dictates of the majority group of the day. There can be no freedom of expression in the full sense unless all facets of life can be portrayed, no matter how repulsive the disclosures may be to some people.

Both the stage and the movies are entitled to the same protection as the lecture platform and the press. They too are media for the communication of ideas—at times the most effective of all. In some nations the theatre has indeed enjoyed a freedom the newspaper has not known. For example, in Indonesia the puppet show is an important vehicle for political satire and for the discussion of public issues. The *dahlong* makes his puppets question, denounce, ridicule, and criticize the various ministries and the laws they enforce. The presence of the minister in the audience quickens, rather than discourages, the criticism. Through the puppets, the *dahlong* can with impunity say things about his government that no editor would undertake to do.

We of the West have developed in a different tradition. We give printing, pamphleteering, and speaking the preferred position because it was around them that our early battles for freedom were fought. The theatre was not important to that struggle. So over the years we developed a different attitude toward it. And when the movies appeared we did not at first put them in the category of the press. The result was that we have had orgies of censorship of the stage that have been more consistent with the totalitarian than with democratic tradition.

Today in England, where freedom of expression occupies a high place, the stage and movies are under strict censorship by the Lord Chamberlain. That system of censorship, which dates back to Henry VIII, once was concerned with slights to the sovereign or with political satire. Later it became concerned with atheism, then with sexual morality, and now seemingly with homosexuality. George Bernard Shaw once summed the matter up as follows: "We have got a censor of plays at present. We have had him for a considerable time. . . . I describe his functions as an unmitigated nuisance. I repeat an unmitigated nuisance. It prevents serious plays from being acted, and consequently prevents them from being written."

Until recently, movies were considered outside the protection of our First Amendment. In 1952, a unanimous Court held that "expression by means of motion pictures is included within the free speech and free press guaranty of the First and Fourteenth Amendments." *Joseph Burstyn Inc.* v. *Wilson*, 343 U.S. 495, 502. I will revert to the problem of censorship later. Suffice it to say at this point that as a matter of principle the stage and the movies are entitled to the same protection of the First Amendment as other methods of expression.

It is my view that protection of the First Amendment also extends to the campaign literature, oratory, advertising, and radio and television broadcasts which accompany the modern political campaign. The First Amendment should give the widest possible protection to the expression of political views. In a democratic society, the expression of a political point of view takes on its greatest significance in connection with the election campaign. Through the ballot box, the views of the majority are given practical significance in the operation of government. And an informed electorate is in turn dependent upon free access to all shades of political opinion. For this reason, it is the very cornerstone of the democratic process that all persons and all groups be allowed to express their views of the fitness of the candidate for office and of the issues for which he stands. For, as Justice Rutledge observed in *United States v. C.I.O.*, 335 U.S. 106, 129, 143, our democratic processes "could hardly go on without" the opportunity for all groups to take their message to the electorate.

And, to be meaningful, the protection of the First Amendment must extend not only to the individual but to all groups in our society. Many individuals and groups in the United States have the power to exert vast pressures in influencing public opinion. The editorial pages of the privately owned metropolitan newspaper, radio and television broadcasts, the pictures and slogans of the advertising agency, the sermon from the pulpit, magazines, books, pamphlets, all have an influence upon public opinion and the outcome of election campaigns.

When it comes to elections there is room, of course, for laws penalizing corrupt practices. Amounts contributed to candidates can be controlled; disclosure of the person or group financing a candidate can be required; and many other campaign activities can be regulated. But at times the regulation has gone further.

Efforts have been made to place restrictions on the amount which certain groups could expend for editorializing their views, announcing them in broadcasts, or expressing them through the ancient method of pamphleteering.

31

The argument has been that if a group spends beyond a certain amount it is exerting an "undue" influence on the community. But that is only an indirect way of silencing speakers or putting them on short rations so far as speaking or writing is concerned. Radio and television time should of course be apportioned so that no one group dominates the air. But apart from this, no control of utterances through control of expenditures would seem permissible.

If it is only necessary that this influence be labeled "undue" to serve as a justification for silencing any person or group, the guarantees of the First Amendment are without substance. Then the newspaper publisher may be forbidden to express his political views on the editorial pages of his newspaper. Then individuals and groups may be forbidden to obtain radio and television time to express opinions as to the fitness of candidates for political office or to discuss election issues. Then the minister may be punished for discussing political matters in his sermons. Then campaign committees may be restricted in expounding their political ideas. But the protection of the First Amendment should not be limited to the orator on a soapbox in a public park. It should extend to every group, large or small, unimportant or influential. It is a constitutional privilege which every person should have, whether he represents business or labor, farmers or financiers, utilities or consumers.

Those who doubt the thesis that man needs full freedom of expression to realize his utmost capacities and become a cultured citizen of the world need only visit the totalitarian states and see how man has shriveled under the impact of censorship, how poorly he has fared under the diet of one creed. The horizons of the citizen in the conformity state are so limited he cannot react intelligently to the world around him. He becomes a victim of the agencies of propaganda which his government manipulates. He is free only in some areas of science such as physics or chemistry, where political ideology does not reach. In the social sciences, in the humanities, in the arts, and perhaps even in agriculture (as Lysenko showed) the scholar in the totalitarian nation is so restricted as to be a mouthpiece for the ruling group.

One need not travel to learn these truths. Kent Cooper in *The Right to Know* has shown the stark tragedies that followed in World War I and World War II when governments ran the news cartels. He has shown in terms of modern history how freedom of expression across the world is essential if there is to be a viable world community. People must have knowledge in order to act intelligently. The standard essential for us in the management of our internal affairs is also essential in the world community. As Article 19 of the Declaration of Human Rights of the United Nations states:

"Everyone has the right to freedom of opinion and expression; this right includes freedom to hold opinions without interference and to seek, receive and impart information and ideas through any media and regardless of frontiers."

There can be no enduring stability in world affairs unless these rights are recognized principles in other lands.

33

When we talk of freedom of expression, we deal then with one of the fundamentals that is important not only to citizenship at home but to membership in the world community.

Freedom of expression has many integrating effects on our own society. The individual who has a Hyde Park where he may blow off steam and rave and rant releases energies that might mount to dangerous proportions if suppressed. A great risk in any age is the tyranny of the majority. Freedom of expression is the weapon of the minority to win over the majority or to temper the policies of those in power. Moreover, freedom of expression makes acquiescence in majority rule more likely. Bryce in *The American Commonwealth* wrote of the therapeutic values of freedom of expression:

"Every view, every line of policy, has its fair chance before the people. No one can say that audience has been denied him, and comfort himself with the hope that, when he is heard, the world will come round to him. Under a repressive government, the sense of grievance and injustice feeds the flame of resistance in a persecuted minority. But in a country like this, where the freedom of the press, the right of public meeting, and the right of association and agitation have been legally extended and are daily exerted more widely than anywhere else in the world, there is nothing to awaken that sense. He whom the multitude condemns or ignores has no further court of appeal to look to. Rome has spoken. His cause has been heard and judgment has gone against him."

The philosophy of the First Amendment is that man must have full freedom to search the world and the universe for the answers to the puzzles of life. In that search the arts and literature may be more important than the dictionary, the morning newspaper, or the encyclopedias. The Jeffersonian faith is that if they are allowed unfettered liberty to accumulate knowledge and in the process even to wallow in trash, if they like, they will acquire the wisdom and ability to manage all of the perplexing and teasing problems of each generation.

Unless the horizons are unlimited, we risk being governed by a set of prejudices of a bygone day. If we are restricted in art, religion, economics, political theory, or any other great field of knowledge, we may become victims of conformity in an age where salvation can be won only by nonconformity.

II. THE CONFLICT BETWEEN FREE EXPRESSION AND OTHER COMMUNITY VALUES

The problem of carrying into practice the philosophy of the First Amendment becomes acute when free expression threatens other community values. There are three main areas in which this conflict is particularly significant today. The first is where speech inflicts injury on individuals. The second, closely related in its history, is where speech endangers law and order or even the security of government itself. The last area is that where speech is thought to undermine community morality.

A. LIBEL AND SLANDER: It is clear that the First Amendment does not give completely free rein to utterances. The Bill of Rights does not underwrite all irresponsible talk. There is intrinsic evidence in the Constitution itself, for Article I Section 6 provides an immunity to Senators and Congressmen for their utterances in Congress: "and for any Speech or Debate in either House, they shall not be questioned in any other Place." This is a right which Peter Wentworth and John Eliot helped Englishmen win. It implies that but for the immunity there might be liability.

It was recognized from the beginning that the First Amendment did not protect one against the penalties for libel and slander. Jefferson in his Second Inaugural Address referred to the calumny suffered by his first administration at the hands of a licentious press and to "the wholesome punishments reserved to and provided by the laws of the several States against falsehood and defamation."

The individual today has recourse to the courts to recover damages for slander or libel. The First Amendment gives no license to defame the citizen. Moreover, there is in our law a criminal as well as a civil sanction against the defamer. These laws, especially in relation to criminal libel, exhibit great differences from State to State. And they represent a long and painful evolution.

This is an evolution that can be characterized in terms of three basic developments—enlargement of the responsi-

36

bility of juries in criminal libel actions, the recognition that truth is a defense, and finally the development of the privilege of fair comment.

We can begin the story with the Star Chamber in England. The Star Chamber—the chief institution for the suppression of religious and political dissenters—punished political libel. Political and religious discussion was repressed on the excuse that suppression was necessary to preserve peace and order, as well as to protect the reputations of prominent people of the realm. The Star Chamber's abuse of its vast powers brought its abolition in 1641. But the law of libel and slander, now the responsibility of the common-law courts, did not grow in an atmosphere which was sympathetic to the value of free discussion. The common-law judges were not champions of freedom of speech or of the press. They developed the rule that publication of any statement scandalous to the government constituted a common-law crime. Truth was no defense in these criminal libel actions. Occasionally, juries would refuse to convict the champion of a popular cause. Accordingly, the courts restricted the jury's role. Juries were instructed that they were to decide only whether the defendant had published the writing with which he was charged. In England, it took Fox's Libel Act of 1792 to give the jury the right to decide whether or not the so-called libel was justified.

The substance of the English law of libel was carried to these shores. In 1735, the court in the famous trial of a New York newspaper publisher, John Peter Zenger, ruled that truth could not justify Zenger's criticism of the Governor of New York. But, contrary to the English practice, the court left to the jury the question whether Zenger's writings tended "to beget an ill opinion" of the government. If so, Zenger was to be found guilty. The jury acquitted. 17 How. St. Tr. 675 (1735). That acquittal marked a milestone in the fight for the right to criticize the government.

The enactment of the First Amendment and of similar free speech guarantees in state constitutions did not immediately change the law of libel. In both the federal and state courts, judges continued to parrot Blackstone's conclusion that liberty of the press is protected only against the imposition of prior restraints upon publication, such as censorship and licensing. The view was that government had an uncontrolled right to punish abuses of speech. But punishment may be as much a deterrent as prior restraint. As Chief Justice Cushing of Massachusetts (later a member of the Supreme Court) wrote John Adams in 1789:

". . . if all men are restrained by the fear of jails, scourges and loss of ears from examining the conduct of persons in administration and where their conduct is illegal, tyrannical and tending to overthrow the Constitution and introduce slavery, are so restrained from declaring it to the public *that* will be as effectual a restraint as any *previous* restraint whatever."

And so the campaign to make truth a defense to libel went forward. The liberty to publish the truth would seem basic to the First Amendment. As Chief Justice Cushing said:

". . . truth sacredly adhered to, can never upon the

whole prejudice right religion, equal government or a government founded upon proper balances and checks, or the happiness of society in any respect, but must be favorable to them all."

Even the infamous and short-lived Sedition Act of 1798, reflecting the growth of American law since the Zenger trial, allowed truth as a defense and permitted the jury to decide all questions, both of law and fact. In civil libel actions, truth was unquestionably a defense at the beginning of the nineteenth century. But there were conflicting decisions concerning the availability of truth as a defense in prosecutions for criminal libel. The issue came to a head, in 1804, in the trial of a newspaper publisher in New York for publishing charges against President Jefferson. *People v. Croswell*, 3 Johns. Cas. 337. The defense urged that liberty of the press demanded the right to speak the truth. Although the New York courts had ruled that truth was no justification, the New York legislature settled the matter, while Croswell's case was still pending, by passing a law allowing the defense. Most legislatures and courts have followed the lead of the New York legislature.

One more battle, however, remained to be fought. Even the defense of truth may not fully serve to protect free discussion. Many matters—such as honesty, integrity, ability—do not yield to nice characterization as true or false. These are matters on which people differ, even where the facts are undisputed. And, in our society, we place a high value on the discussion of affairs of public interest. Thus, beginning in the middle of the nineteenth century, the priv-

39

ilege of fair comment began to take form. Fair comment, even today, is a privilege which exhibits great diversities in our state courts. For that reason, a detailed discussion of its complexities is out of place here. Basically, however, the privilege of fair comment is aimed at immunizing from the rigors of the law of libel and slander comment upon facts of public interest, such as the conduct of government affairs and the fitness of a candidate for public office, regardless of truth or falsity. It can best be illustrated by noting the statement of a New York court discussing the privilege in 1942. The court said in *Hall* v. *Binghamton Press Co.*, 263 App. Div. 403, 411:

"In times like those through which we have recently passed, the doctrine of fair comment should be extended as far as the authorities will permit. With unprecedented social and governmental conditions, our own institutions threatened, national legislators who participate in the formation of governmental policies should be held to the strictest official accountability. History has shown that this is promoted through free exercise of the right to criticize official acts. The people furnish the legislators with an extensive and expensive secretariat, give them the right to use the mails at public expense. Their colleagues are generous in granting leave to print. With these opportunities for personal praise and propaganda, opposition newspapers and editorial writers should not be limited to weak, tepid and supine criticism and discussion."

This approach reflects the true spirit of the Bill of Rights.

The history of libel is very important as indicating some of the evils and excesses which the Bill of Rights sought to avoid. As Mr. Justice Black wrote in *Bridges* v. *California*, 314 U.S. 252, 265:

> "Ratified as it was while the memory of many oppressive English restrictions on the enumerated liberties was still fresh, the First Amendment cannot reasonably be taken as approving prevalent English practices. On the contrary, the only conclusion supported by history is that the unqualified prohibitions laid down by the framers were intended to give to liberty of the press, as to the other liberties, the broadest scope that could be countenanced in an orderly society."

Criminal libel presents dangerous potentialities. All the States punish libels directed at individuals. A few do so without legislative enactment. Most have statutes defining the crime. It is "a malicious defamation" which either impeaches the "virtue" of a person or tends to bring him into "public ridicule." And some States extend the protection to groups as well as to individuals.

The problem is especially important where public officials are concerned or where public matters are involved. As I have said, one main function of the First Amendment is to ensure ample opportunity for the people to determine and resolve public issues. Where public matters are involved, the doubts should be resolved in favor of freedom of expression rather than against it. Otherwise criminal libel will tend to cast the same shadow over discussion of public affairs as seditious libel once did. The extreme to which the prosecutions have gone is shown in *State* v. *Haffer*, 94 Wash. 136, where a conviction was sustained against a man who exposed the memory of George Washington to hatred, contempt, and obloquy.

Criminal libel is not extensively used, if one is to judge by the reported cases. But a majority of those that are reported in the last two decades are in the public domain. That is to say, they deal with charges against public officials—charges of malfeasance, dishonesty, incompetency. Many of these suits serve the end once served by seditious libel: to protect "the great men of the realm," in the words of an ancient British statute. If seditious libel is not to creep back into the law under the guise of criminal libel, the citizen must have large leeway in making "fair comment" on the conduct and attitudes of those who sit in the seats of government and on every issue that is a matter of community concern.

The law of criminal libel has deep tap roots in history. One of the original justifications for it was the tendency of defamations of character to cause a breach of the peace. Today the element of breach of the peace is omitted from most of the statutes governing criminal libel. But courts continue to rely on that element to justify convictions.

When breach of the peace is considered, the question of proximity and degree becomes important. A particular libel should not be condemned merely because libels sometimes cause breaches of the peace or are apt to do so, but because this particular libel was comparable to striking a match in a place filled with gasoline fumes. Unless the rights of free speech and free press are closely guarded and allowed to be qualified or denied only in case a breach of the peace is immediate, the police power, rather than the First Amendment, will become preferred in our constitutional system. Yet the command of the First Amendment is unequivocal—"Congress shall make no law . . . abridging the freedom of speech, or of the press."

Unfortunately, that has not been the drift of the decisions. The trend has been to penalize certain utterances even without any showing of an immediacy of injury which the speech would cause the other interests of government.

A graphic example is *Beauharnais* v. *Illinois*, 343 U.S. 250. That was a prosecution for group libel under an Illinois statute. Those said to be libeled were Negroes. The defendant was a member of a group that sponsored a species of white supremacy. He called upon the "one million self respecting white people in Chicago to unite . . ." so as to halt the invasion of white neighborhoods by Negroes. His rallying call was centered around a sentence in his lithograph which said, "If persuasion and the need to prevent the white race from becoming mongrelized by the Negro will not unite us, then the aggressions . . . rapes, robberies, knives, guns and marijuana of the Negro surely will." The leaflets were distributed on Chicago street corners. A divided Court sustained a judgment of conviction. The majority, speaking through Mr. Justice Frankfurter, held that talk such as this played "a significant part" in creating tensions between the races that on other occasions had resulted in race riots. But the Court did not require any showing that this leaflet in the context of its distribution created any immediate danger of conflict and violence.

43

That question was said to be irrelevant to the problem. It was said to be irrelevant because libelous statements were not "within the area of constitutionally protected speech." *Id.*, p. 266. Thus libel is outlawed because it tends to incite breaches of the peace; yet no opportunity is granted to show that a particular libel has no likelihood of producing that result.

The consequence is that the First Amendment is made subordinate to the police power. This is dangerous doctrine. It means that the rule which puts the white man in jail for criticizing the invasion by Negroes into white communities in the North can put the Negro in jail for criticizing lynching or segregation in the South. If such talk is apt to produce conflict and discord, it can be banned. The judgment of the legislature is made supreme. In dealing with speech, the legislature is allowed the same leeway it enjoys when dealing with problems of housing, wages, hours of work, and the closed shop. Freedom of expression —though preferred in our scheme of things by virtue of the strictness of the command of the First Amendment—loses that preferred position and becomes subject to such "reasonable regulation" as judges from time to time approve.

That is, in other words, an application of the standard of "due process" contained in the Fifth and Fourteenth Amendments. These Amendments insure that a man's life, liberty, or property will not be taken without due process of law. What is "due process"? Due process requires that the legislature act not without reason, not capriciously. This is a standard foreign to the First Amendment—an Amendment designed by its framers to take from government the power to decide when expression may "reasonably" be suppressed. For that reason, I disagree with the view of Judge Learned Hand that the prohibitions of the First Amendment, in terms absolute, are "no more than admonitions of moderation." Hand, *The Spirit of Liberty* (2d ed., 1953), p. 278. The idea that they are no more than that has done more to undermine liberty in this country than any other single force. That notion is, indeed, at the root of the forces of disintegration that have been eroding the democratic ideal in this country.

B. THREATS TO LAW AND ORDER AND GOVERNMENT SECURITY: The *Beauharnais* decision is a throwback to the oppressive days when seditious libel was used to stamp out talk believed dangerous to government. Dangerous talk has been the bane of every uneasy ruler. Dangerous talk was the excuse for oppression in our colonial days, an excuse that has had many distinguished proponents. One was Samuel Johnson, who thought that "no member of a society has a right to *teach* any doctrine contrary to what the society holds to be true." He said:

"Every society has a right to preserve public peace and order, and therefore has a good right to prohibit the propagation of opinions which have a dangerous tendency. . . . He may be morally or theologically wrong in restraining the propagation of opinions which he thinks dangerous; but he is politically right."

The beginning of our experience under the First Amendment was not auspicious: laws were soon enacted to punish

45

talk thought likely to undermine the government. In 1798 the Alien and Sedition Laws were passed making it a crime, among other things, to publish any "false, scandalous and malicious writing" against the government, the Congress, or the President with intent to defame them or bring them into "contempt or disrepute" or "to stir up sedition." The fear was of the French and their espionage here. This was a short-lived law, lasting by its terms only until 1801 and never extended. But it brought a reign of terror to the nation. Matthew Lyon of Vermont was fined and imprisoned for criticizing President Adams and condemning his policy toward France. Thomas Cooper was fined and imprisoned for criticizing Adams for delivering up an American citizen to the British Navy for court-martial. Anthony Haswell of Vermont was fined and imprisoned for denouncing the political persecution of Matthew Lyon. James T. Callender of Virginia was fined and imprisoned for criticizing Adams and accusing him of attempting to embroil this country with France. He wrote, "Take your choice, then, between Adams, war and beggary, and Jefferson, peace and competency." David Brown was fined and imprisoned for proclaiming against those oppressive laws and saying "Downfall to the tyrants of America: peace and retirement to the President: long live the Vice President and the minority." Luther Baldwin was fined for a comment he made when a cannon was fired in Adams' honor. Baldwin was heard to say that he hoped the wadding behind the powder would hit Adams in the seat of his pants.

During the trials under the Alien and Sedition Laws,

counsel for the defendants got nowhere with their objections to the validity of these Acts. The power of the federal judiciary to declare Acts of Congress unconstitutional was not announced until 1803 when *Marbury* v. *Madison*, 1 Cranch 137, was decided. In the earlier reign of terror caused by the Alien and Sedition Laws, the federal courts undertook only to enforce them, not to pass on their validity. Those laws would not, of course, pass judicial scrutiny today, as Justice Holmes indicated in his dissent in *Abrams* v. *United States*, 250 U.S. 616, 630, since they would strike at the very heart of free political comment.

We atoned as a nation for the injustices perpetrated under the Alien and Sedition Laws. When Jefferson was elected in the 1800 campaign, he promptly pardoned those who had been convicted for seditious utterance; and for the next fifty years Congress passed laws remitting the fines of those who had been convicted.

Any law forbidding criticism of the government is at war with the First Amendment.

The Court first addressed itself to this problem in 1919 in the case of *Schenck* v. *United States*, 249 U.S. 47. That decision sustained the convictions of those who, during World War I, distributed pamphlets, appealing to young men not to submit to induction into the Armed Forces. Mr. Justice Holmes wrote for the Court, saying in the *Schenck* case:

> "When a nation is at war many things that might be said in time of peace are such a hindrance to its effort that their utterance will not be endured so long as men

47

fight and that no Court could regard them as protected by any Constitutional right." *Id.*, p. 52.

The war power is a pervasive one. Yet even the drastic exigencies of the war power do not easily justify restrictions on the communication of ideas. Mr. Justice Holmes defined the limits beyond which Congress could not go to limit the bounds of free discussion, even under its power to make war.

> "The most stringent protection of speech would not protect a man in falsely shouting fire in a theatre and causing a panic. It does not even protect a man from an injunction against uttering words that may have all the effect of force. . . . The question in every case is whether the words used are used in such circumstances and are of such a nature as to create a clear and present danger that they will bring about the substantive evils that Congress has a right to prevent." *Id.*, p. 52.

This admonition, that speech was not subject to criminal penalties solely because Congress has a *right to prevent the course of conduct* which speech advocates, was soon to be ignored by the Court.

The precedent of the *Schenck* case was applied to sustain convictions in *Abrams* v. *United States*, 250 U.S. 616, a holding reminiscent of earlier seditious libel prosecutions. The accused distributed circulars opposing the war and in substance calling for a general strike. The Court ruled that an anti-war speech in the midst of war was a transgression which Congress could punish, regardless of the immediacy of any threat of success. This led Mr. Justice Holmes, with whom Mr. Justice Brandeis concurred, to dissent:

". . . when men have realized that time has upset many fighting faiths, they may come to believe even more than they believe the very foundations of their own conduct that the ultimate good desired is better reached by free trade in ideas—that the best test of truth is the power of the thought to get itself accepted in the competition of the market, and that truth is the only ground upon which their wishes safely can be carried out. That at any rate is the theory of our Constitution." *Id.*, p. 630.

In a later case Mr. Justice Holmes, speaking for himself and Mr. Justice Brandeis, admonished the Court that for the utterance to be punished, even in time of war, the danger from the speech must be "clear and present," not "remote or possible." *Schaeffer* v. *United States*, 251 U.S. 466, 486.

But the majority of the Court did not apply the clear and present danger test narrowly and critically.

With the end of World War I, some States initiated prosecutions under statutes which made it criminal to advocate overthrow of the government by violent means. The majority of the Court indicated that it placed beyond the pale ideas which included advocacy of the violent overthrow of organized government. Such were the views expressed in *Gitlow* v. *New York*, 268 U.S. 652, where the Court sustained a conviction of communists prosecuted under a state law for advocating overthrow of the government by force and violence. The judgment of the legislature that these utterances were dangerous was given well-nigh conclusive weight. The element of immediacy of danger from the speech was in effect discarded.

In the *Gitlow* case Mr. Justice Holmes, in a dissent in which Mr. Justice Brandeis joined, pleaded for a strict showing of dangerous tendency:

". . . But whatever may be thought of the redundant discourse before us it had no chance of starting a present conflagration. If in the long run the beliefs expressed in proletarian dictatorship are destined to be accepted by the dominant forces of the community, the only meaning of free speech is that they should be given their chance and have their way." *Id.*, p. 673.

In 1951 *Dennis* v. *United States*, 341 U.S. 494, was decided. The leading communists in this country went on trial under a federal law which made it a crime to advocate or teach the desirability of the overthrow of the government by force or violence. A divided Court upheld the conviction on a record which showed advocacy of revolution through use of the classical literature of communism containing the creed of forceful overthrow of existing government. The majority concluded that Congress had the power to punish such utterances where the intent was present to overthrow the government "as speedily as circumstances would permit." *Id.*, p. 510.

But there was no evidence that these defendants had conspired to overthrow the government. Mere agreement to meet in the future to teach and advocate violent subversion was the crime. Yet in the United States in the early

1950's there was no remote possibility that the government or the existing economic structure would then, or in the foreseeable future, be overturned by violent or illegal means. Then, as now, communists in the United States were the peddlers of unwanted ideas. They were more thoroughly investigated and exposed than any group in our history. They were the most unpopular people in the land, incapable of commanding enough votes to get elected to any office, no matter how lowly. Yet the Court sanctioned the suppression of speech which Congress had determined to be "dangerous."

These decisions do not square with the First Amendment. The correct principle was stated by Jefferson, who wrote in 1786, ". . . it is time enough for the rightful purposes of civil government, for its office to interfere when principles break out into overt acts against peace and good order." As Clarence Darrow once said, "There is no such crime as a crime of thought; there are only crimes of action."

The instances in which the Court has been most faithful to the constitutional prohibition against punishment for utterances involve newspaper publications concerning court proceedings. This is the area known as contempt by publication. Until the 1940's, the rule had been that a federal judge could summarily punish for contempt a newspaper editor who published an article critical of the court in a pending case if the publication had a "reasonable tendency" to obstruct the administration of justice. See *Toledo Newspaper Company* v. *United States*, 247 U.S. 402, 421. In 1941, the *Toledo* case was overruled, the Court

51

holding that under the Act of Congress vesting federal courts with contempt power, publications could not be punished summarily by federal judges. *Nye* v. *United States*, 313 U.S. 33.

That case was shortly followed by a series of cases from the States in which the Court, relying on the First Amendment, narrowly restricted the contempt power when directed toward newspapers. The Court in reversing judgments of conviction applied the "clear and present danger" test in the strict fashion which Holmes and Brandeis had advocated. The "evil" with which the States were dealing was twofold: disrespect for the judiciary; and disorderly and unfair administration of justice. The first was held to have no relevancy to the problem, the Court saying, "The assumption that respect for the judiciary can be won by shielding judges from published criticism wrongly appraises the character of American public opinion. For it is a prized American privilege to speak one's mind, although not always with perfect good taste, on all public institutions." *Bridges* v. *California*, 314 U.S. 252, 270. As stated in *Craig* v. *Harney*, 331 U.S. 367, 376, "Judges are supposed to be men of fortitude, able to thrive in a hardy climate." If they are defamed, they may seek redress in the civil courts as other citizens may do.

The prevention of disorderly and unfair administration of justice is, of course, an "evil" which rightly concerns the state; and measures can be adopted to protect the integrity of trials. For example, a trial dominated by a mob is no trial by American standards of due process. *Moore* v. *Dempsey*, 261 U.S. 86. Newspapers by screaming headlines, inflammatory news accounts, and demanding editorials can create a climate of opinion in which no fair trial of the defendant can be had. As stated by the Court in the *Bridges* case, "Legal trials are not like elections, to be won through the use of the meeting-hall, the radio, and the newspaper." 314 U.S., p. 271. Newspaper comment may create such a hostile atmosphere as to make necessary a removal of the trial to another forum. Newspaper comment could be "so designed and executed as to poison the public mind, to cause a march on the courthouse, or otherwise so disturb the delicate balance in a highly wrought situation as to imperil the fair and orderly functioning of the judicial process," and empower the judge to punish for contempt. *Craig* v. *Harney*, 331 U.S., p. 375. Short of such dire consequences, newspaper comment on judges or on particular cases may proceed with immunity from the contempt power. For unless immediate and substantial impairment of a fair and orderly trial is threatened, there is no "clear and present danger" which authorizes government to take action abridging freedom of the press.

In this one sector of the First Amendment the Court has adhered faithfully to the Holmes-Brandeis conception of "clear and present danger." In the main, the Court has departed substantially from it. The result has been that legislatures more and more regulate speech. Speech becomes subordinate to the police power and is regulated in the manner of housing and industrial accidents.

From *Schenck* to *Dennis*, I know of no abridgment of freedom of expression which was properly sustained under the "clear and present danger" test. Being of the generation

53

of young men called to service in World War I, I cannot
conceive that the pamphlets which Schenck distributed
had any measurable effect upon the conduct of the war
effort. Being close to American affairs in the 1950's, I cannot conceive that the communist's advocacy of the violent
overthrow of government has convinced more than a hand-
ful of the American public. "Clear and present danger" has
become merely a convenient excuse for suppression. Yet in
my view the only time suppression is constitutionally justified is where speech is so closely brigaded with action
that it is in essence a part of an overt act.

It is not enough that the words excite people or cause
unrest or disturbance. As the Court said in *Terminiello* v.
Chicago, 337 U.S. 1, 4:

> ". . . a function of free speech under our system of gov-
> ernment is to invite dispute. It may indeed best serve
> its high purpose when it induces a condition of unrest,
> creates dissatisfaction with conditions as they are, or
> even stirs people to anger. Speech is often provocative
> and challenging. It may strike at prejudices and pre-
> conceptions and have profound unsettling effects as it
> presses for acceptance of an idea."

Speech may, of course, be so close a companion of action
as to be an overt act, as when fire is shouted in a crowded
theatre. But the First Amendment should let people talk,
no matter how provocative the words may be, unless they
are a part of action which the government is authorized
to control.

Picketing is an outstanding example. In 1940, the Court

decided that picketing, as a means by which organized labor publicizes its views in a labor dispute, was entitled to First Amendment protection. Accordingly, a statute which placed a flat ban on all picketing was overturned. But picketing involves more than free speech. Organized patrolling of the employer's place of business may present traffic problems, and even questions of law and order, such as fist fights and violence. These are matters with which the States are clearly empowered to deal. Thus the Court has held that all picketing may be prohibited when it has been characterized by outbreaks of violence. And picketing is also a method of asserting economic pressure on the picketed concern—a method which may in particular instances be fully as effective as a strike or a boycott. Picketing brigaded with a course of conduct seeking an unlawful economic objective can be regulated or prohibited. In *Giboney* v. *Empire Storage Co.*, 336 U.S. 490, for example, a concern was picketed to compel it to become a party to an unlawful combination in restraint of trade. Picketing there was held to have been properly prohibited, because it was used "as an integral part of conduct in violation of a valid criminal statute." *Id.*, p. 498. The Court has emphasized more and more the non-speech aspects of picketing. As shown by *Teamsters Union* v. *Vogt,* 354 U.S. 284, the Court has permitted the regulation of picketing in much the same way that the States and Congress can regulate any other aspect of the collective bargaining relationship. In this it would seem the Court has erred. Picketing, when freed from conduct that the law can reach, should stand immune from prohibition since it is a method of expression.

Speeches by an employer to his employees are another example. Although an employer, no less than an employee, is fully protected by the First Amendment, his communications to his employees also take on the character of something more than speech. Just as picketing may be a device to assert economic pressure, the employer's speech to his employees may, in context, amount to a threat of discharge, if the employer's expressed wishes are ignored. When the totality of an employer's course of conduct operates to coerce his employees, the fact that this conduct is evidenced in part by speech does not immunize it from regulation or prohibition. Then the employer's speech is brigaded with conduct—coercion of his employees—which the legislature has the power to prohibit. As Mr. Justice Murphy said in *Labor Board* v. *Virginia Power Co.*, 314 U.S. 469, 477, ". . . conduct, though evidenced in part by speech, may amount, in connection with other circumstances, to coercion . . ."; and coercive conduct by an employer towards his employees is not protected by the First Amendment.

Another classical case is the use of "fighting" words—"those which by their very utterance inflict injury or tend to incite an immediate breach of the peace." *Chaplinsky* v. *New Hampshire,* 315 U.S. 568, 572.

In this field of fighting words, the Court has greatly enlarged the category of unprotected speech. *Feiner* v. *New York*, 340 U.S. 315, is an example. Feiner, a university student, made a street-corner speech, standing on a box and using loudspeakers, in a colored residential section. He made derogatory remarks about the President, the Mayor, and the American Legion. He told his audience of seventy-five people, both white and colored, that the Negroes should fight for equal rights they had been denied. There was some pushing, shoving, and muttering in the crowd. After Feiner had been speaking for twenty minutes, a man approached the two police officers on the scene and threatened to pull Feiner off the platform if the police did not. At this point, Feiner was ordered to stop speaking and arrested when he refused. He was convicted for inciting a breach of the peace and the Court upheld the conviction. Feiner was silenced because his audience was unsympathetic and because one man had threatened to haul him from the stage. The police were permitted to weigh the advantages and disadvantages of allowing him to speak. They were allowed to silence the speaker, rather than protect him.

The Court forgot the teaching of Mr. Justice Brandeis in *Whitney* v. *California,* 274 U.S. 354, 377, that, "If there be time to expose through discussion the falsehood and fallacies, to avert the evil by the processes of education, the remedy to be applied is more speech, not enforced silence."

Once the streets or parks are used for speaking or distributing literature, special problems may be created. The grant of an unlimited discretion to an official to allow or disallow a meeting on public property has the same vice as a system of licensing the press or speech. Freedom of

57

assembly is a part of the First Amendment and as important to freedom of expression as free speech or free press themselves. As Chief Justice Hughes said in *De Jonge* v. *Oregon*, 299 U.S. 353, 364, "The right of peaceable assembly is a right cognate to those of free speech and free press and is equally fundamental." So long as the meeting is orderly and lawful, the right of assembly cannot be denied because the people gathering there are communists or members of other despised groups.

But the gathering of people together often creates problems which, though incidental to freedom of expression and freedom of assembly, must be subject to some control in the interests of peace and quiet or law and order. Two cases will illustrate the two extremes. In *Cox* v. *New Hampshire*, 312 U.S. 569, the requirements for a license to hold a parade in connection with the dissemination of views was sustained, the licensing system being designed to control traffic conditions without discrimination. Traffic congestion is a legitimate concern of any city. That problem need not bow to unrestricted freedom of expression. As Chief Justice Hughes said, "One would not be justified in ignoring the familiar red traffic light because he thought it his religious duty to disobey the municipal command or sought by that means to direct public attention to an announcement of his opinions." *Id.*, p. 574.

At the other extreme are ordinances forbidding the use of sound amplification devices in public places without the permission of the chief of police who has the discretion to grant or deny permission as he chooses. Those ordinances were held unconstitutional as a prior restraint in *Saia* v. *New York*, 334 U.S. 558. The Court said:

"Noise can be regulated by regulating decibels. The hours and place of public discussion can be controlled. But to allow the police to bar the use of loud-speakers because their use can be abused is like barring radio receivers because they too make a noise. The police need not be given the power to deny a man the use of his radio in order to protect a neighbor against sleepless nights." *Id.*, p. 562.

The police power of local governments can reach such things as noise, riots, and traffic jams. It cannot, however, reach freedom of expression. If, therefore, a meeting, a lecture, or a speech presents problems of noise, riots, or traffic jams the latter can be regulated even in the form of licensing. But lest the regulation in the interest of noise, riot, or traffic control be used as a cloak to control freedom of expression or have that effect, the Court has insisted that the regulation be "narrowly drawn to prevent the supposed evil." *Cantwell* v. *Connecticut*, 310 U.S. 296, 307.

c. OBSCENITY: A word should be said about obscenity. Though the law reports are filled with decisions on the subject, very few of them deal with the First Amendment aspects of the problem.

The dangers to freedom of expression inherent in our obscenity laws are the same dangers which inhere in any governmental attempt to censor literature and the arts. Under the guise of protecting the public from obscenity, the government may decide what books the public may safely read, which motion pictures the public may safely see. Obscenity is a slippery term. The very vagueness of the obscenity concept can permit public officials to brand books as obscene merely because they question contemporary moral standards or accepted religious principles. Various public and private groups in this country have exerted tremendous pressures against those who distribute books which the group has labeled as "offensive" or "objectionable." Ostensibly, some groups seek to protect youth or an abnormal mind from literature which portrays acts of crime or sex. Too often, however, a book finds its way to a censor's black list solely because it offends the censor's own moral sensibilities, or reflects a moral code with which the censor disagrees. Other groups seek to reduce all literature to a children's nursery level of inoffensiveness.

One occasionally reads that if a court or a legislature attaches the word "obscene" to a publication it is placed beyond constitutional protection. There was such a suggestion in *Beauharnais* v. *Illinois,* 343 U.S. 250, 266, and it is, I think, fallacious. Obscenity deals primarily with the problems of publications concerning sex. To put a ban on sex literature because, regardless of its overall literary or educational value, it has salacious passages, would be to inflict a prudish, Victorian regime on our communities. Sex cannot be suppressed in literature any more than it can in life. Sex problems and sex behavior are as much entitled to the protection of the First Amendment as the misery of the poor or the extravagances of the rich. If there is to be intelligence in coming to grips with the problems of sex, there must be the widest possible discussion of it and dissemination of views concerning it. *Winters* v. *New York*, 333 U.S. 507, 510, said that literature dealing with lust and crime was entitled to constitutional protection. There is no reason why sex literature should be less favorably treated.

The words commonly used—obscene, lurid, lascivious, filthy, indecent, and disgusting—have had a long use in the history of criminal law in the Western world. The major constitutional problems come with their application.

There are at times suggestions that a work is obscene which challenges the accepted moral standards of the community. That is in essence the test adopted by the Court in *Roth* v. *United States*, 354 U.S. 476. Such a broad definition of obscenity flies in the face of the First Amendment, one of whose purposes is that through talk and debate, rather than through suppression, we seek to perfect our lives. If there were not this leeway in the moral as well as in the political and social field, we would restrict freedom of expression to propaganda supporting not change, but the *status quo*. One might as well bar publications offensive to people as to bar those that challenge our accustomed morality. Yet if one started out to bar that which is offensive to the community, he would give the censors free reign.

Obscenity is sometimes defined to include that which arouses thoughts about sex. In *Roth* v. *United States*, 354 U.S. 476, the Court sustained a conviction for obscenity which was defined to mean a publication which has "a substantial tendency to deprave or corrupt its readers by inciting lascivious thoughts or arousing lustful desires." The idea of using obscenity to bar thoughts of sex is dangerous. A person without sex thoughts is abnormal. Sex thoughts may induce sex practices that make for better marital relations. Sex thoughts that make love attractive certainly should not be outlawed. If the illicit is included, that should make no constitutional difference. For education concerning the illicit may well stimulate people to seek their experiences in wedlock rather than out of it.

As Judge Jerome Frank stated in *Roth* v. *Goldman,* 172 F. 2d 788, 792, "I think that no sane man thinks socially dangerous the arousing of normal sexual desires. Consequently, if reading obscene books has merely that consequence, Congress, it would seem, can constitutionally no more suppress books than it can prevent the mailing of many other objects, such as perfumes, for example, which notoriously produce that result."

I can understand (and at times even sympathize) with programs of school groups and church groups to protect and defend the existing moral standards of the community. I can understand the motives of the Anthony Comstocks who would impose Victorian standards on the community. I can tolerate (though not respect) the activities of busybodies who seek to impose their own morality on others. In the obscenity cases we are not concerned with the advocacy of private groups. Here we are concerned with the extent, if any, to which government may step in and stop publications or punish the publishers or distributors. The question is whether government can espouse one moral code as against another and apply sanctions against those who write or speak against the norm. It is my view that the First Amendment permits government to be concerned only with anti-social conduct, not with utterances.

We know precious little about the effect of sex literature on conduct. There is doubt if it has any appreciable effect on juvenile delinquency. It is significant that the Gluecks, in their exhaustive survey of the numerous factors that bear on juvenile delinquency, do not list the things that the juveniles read. Glueck, *Unraveling Juvenile Delinquency* (1950). Yet if there is a constitutional basis for punishing the publication of obscene literature, it must be because it is clear that the obscene publication causes anti-social conduct, not among psychopaths, but among the average of the group to which it is addressed.

Regina v. *Hicklin*, LR 3 Q B 360, 371 (1868), gave as the test of obscenity "whether the tendency of the matter charged as obscenity is to deprave and corrupt those whose minds are open to such immoral influences, and into whose hands a publication of this sort may fall." This view, which became finally accepted in this country, tested literature by its effects on the psychopaths. It pandered to the hyper-sensitive and stifled the artists. It allowed thought to be fettered "by the necessities of the lowest and least capable." *United States* v. *Kennerley*, 209 F. 119, 121. It could not, therefore, pass scrutiny under the First Amendment.

Similarly, there are statements that courts should define obscenity by determining what literature children can safely read. This is the standard the Court recently struck down in *Butler* v. *Michigan*, 352 U.S. 380. Butler was convicted, for selling a book to a Detroit policeman, under a

Michigan statute which made it a crime to distribute to the general reading public a book found to have a potentially deleterious influence on youth. In reversing his conviction, the Court, speaking through Mr. Justice Frankfurter, said: "The incidence of this enactment is to reduce the adult population of Michigan to reading only what is fit for children." That a particular publication may not be fit for the eyes of children cannot form the constitutional basis for banning its distribution to adults.

Some courts have condemned, as obscene, books which were only partly such. The decision in *United States* v. *One Book Entitled Ulysses,* 72 F. 2d 705, reversed this trend by holding that in determining whether a book is obscene it must be considered as a whole. It is the "dominant effect" of the book that is controlling. *Id.,* p. 708. The court went on to say: "In applying this test, relevancy of the objectionable parts to the theme, the established reputation of the work in the estimation of approved critics, if the book is modern, and the verdict of the past, if it is ancient, are persuasive pieces of evidence; for works of art are not likely to sustain a high position with no better warrant for their existence than their obscene content." The Court recently adopted as the controlling test the dominant effect of the book as a whole. *Roth* v. *United States,* 354 U.S. 476.

In determining whether a particular publication causes anti-social conduct, a number of factors become relevant. The effect of the publication as a whole is one consideration. The fact that the publication is "designed merely to catch the prurient" (*United States* v. *Rebhuhn,* 109 F. 2d 512, 514) is of importance. The fact that the selling campaign is aimed at juveniles may likewise be relevant. The medium of expression used may also make a vital difference. What appears in cold print may be innocuous while the same theme vividly portrayed in movies might propel people into action.

Though the law of obscenity has an ancient lineage, it is only now being defined in terms of the First Amendment. Certainly the common test suggested by courts—whether the publication arouses sexual thoughts—cannot be squared with the First Amendment. A state of mind is not enough; it is the relationship of that state of mind to overt action that would seem to be critical.

By this test it is unlikely that many publications designed for general distribution would fall under the ban. That seems to be the necessary consequence, if we are to adhere to the First Amendment. That Amendment does not guarantee freedom of the press to publications only when they contain inoffensive material. The First Amendment contains a much broader guarantee. It speaks in absolute terms. It should be respected even when we come to offensive material, unless there is such a close nexus between the words and anti-social action that the two can be said to be brigaded. The excesses that must be tolerated will bring less evil than the institution of a regime of censors looking for material that is offensive.

This approach, however, has not been followed by the Court. The definition of obscenity recently adopted relates the test not to anti-social conduct but to offensiveness. In *Roth* v. *United States*, 354 U.S. 476, it said, "Obscene material is material which deals with sex in a manner appealing to prurient interests." But the Court went on to say, "The portrayal of sex, e.g. in art, literature and scientific works, is not itself sufficient reason to deny material the constitutional protection of freedom of speech and press. Sex, a great and mysterious motive force in human life, has indisputably been a subject of absorbing interest to mankind through the ages; it is one of the vital problems of human interest and public concern."

The approach taken by a majority of the Court departs substantially, I think, from the ideal. But the Court has emphasized that sex is a legitimate subject of discussion, and that the First Amendment cannot be deemed entirely inapplicable to literature dealing with sex. The Court has insisted too that it is the effect of the material as a whole upon normal persons in the community that is to be judged, rather than the effect of isolated excerpts upon particularly susceptible persons. Although I believe that the Court has not acted in this area to give literature the full protection it deserves under the First Amendment, the safeguards which the Court has seen fit to impose are important ones.

III. CENSORSHIP AND PRIOR RESTRAINT

Censorship or prior restraint is anathema to the First Amendment, for it puts the hand of the censor in every editorial and in every news account. Once the censor enters the scene, he becomes by virtue of his power the dictator. One cannot engage in litigation over every editorial or news account as to which the author and the censor differ. The date of publication presses for release of news and editorials. The practical exigencies of a system of censorship means that the author writes to the standards of the censor, who is beyond effective control. He writes to avoid the censor's prejudices and displeasure, if not to please him. The censor becomes the great leveler of thought. The censor sets a deadening pattern of conformity which one must meet or go out of business.

Moreover, jurisdiction feeds on itself and tends to expand. A censor's duty is to censor; and he is subject to the pressures of special groups demanding suppression. The tendency, I think, is for the censor to construe his powers liberally and freely and to expand his jurisdiction until he ends in stupid and silly rulings that often make his role a laughingstock. Milton in *Areopagitica* put his finger on this aspect of the problem when he wrote that there was no "more tedious and unpleasing journey-work" than a censor's job; that, therefore, we must expect the censor to be "either ignorant, imperious, and remiss, or basely pecuniary." He went on to say, "Truth and understanding are not such wares as to be monopolized and traded in by tickets and statutes, and standards." Yet through the ages conformity has been the great desire of every censor and his own jurisdiction an ever-broadening one.

Prior restraint, as contrasted to punishment for publication of illegal works, has other evils. Prosecution for what has been published requires much work and effort by the prosecutor. The censor need only use one stroke of the pen. A system of prior restraint makes it more likely that rulings adverse to freedom of expression will be made than does a system of subsequent punishment. Prior restraint gives the advantage to those who would suppress freedom of the press. Under a system of subsequent punishment, the advantage is with the author, editor, and publisher. A censor can always find what he's looking for, especially when he's looking for smut or earmarks of disloyalty.

Under a system of prior restraint the citizen loses many advantages he enjoys under a system of subsequent punishment. The system of prior restraint is an administrative one. Judicial review is narrow and limited and frequently impossible to obtain. Prior restraint tends to make the bureaucracy supreme. A system of subsequent punishment gives the citizen protection that prior restraint denies—the duty of the government to prove guilt beyond a reasonable doubt, a presumption of innocence, stricter rules of evidence, a challenge to the law on the grounds of vagueness, and a jury trial. These safeguards are not negligible. They are part of our hard-won rights against government that over and again has proved to be obnoxiously officious.

Moreover, a judicial proceeding airs the merits as well as the demerits of a book. Censors do not like publicity. They prefer to work in secret, promulgating their decrees by easy strokes of the pen, and censoring work by work or *en masse* as the spirit moves.

These are some of the great vices of censorship and prior restraint that put them at war with the First Amendment.

The law involved in *Near* v. *Minnesota*, 283 U.S. 697,

worked a prior restraint in a modern setting. The English-speaking world had had a special history of the prior restraint. Henry VIII put the entire press under a licensing system. Before one could publish he had to submit his intended work to the government for approval. This licensing system persisted in England until 1695. The Minnesota law, which came before the Court in 1931 in the *Near* case, carried the prior restraint one step further. A publisher who had a record of publishing "malicious, scandalous, and defamatory" material was put out of business completely. And scandalous and defamatory matter was defined as including charges against public officers of official dereliction, even though true. In a decision that is one of the great landmarks of freedom of the press, the Court held the Minnesota law unconstitutional as embodying "the essence of censorship." *Id.*, p. 713. Under the American system it would be unthinkable that a paper or magazine would first have to submit its pages to a censor before it could publish them. Yet if the government could close the paper or magazine down because of its tendency to publish stories that the government deemed dangerous or obnoxious, an indirect censorship would be attained, as Chief Justice Hughes said.

The power to stop the distribution of literature is as powerful a prior restraint as one imposed on the printing itself. Liberty of circulation is as much a part of freedom of the press as liberty of publication.

Historically, many literary purges have been conducted by tyrannical majorities. A religious group has often been strong enough to gain the support of judges in punishing the publication of books critical of the sect. Purity leagues have succeeded in banning such books as Theodore Dreiser's *An American Tragedy* and Edmund Wilson's *Memoirs of Hecate County.* Federal officials, sitting astride the shipment of second-class mail, have sometimes been prone to act as censors. *Hannegan* v. *Esquire,* 327 U.S. 146. The Supreme Court in striking down the attempted censorship in the *Esquire* case said: "Under our system of government there is an accommodation for the widest varieties of tastes and ideas. What is good literature, what has educational value, what is refined public information, what is good art, varies with individuals as it does from one generation to another. There doubtless would be a contrariety of views concerning Cervantes' *Don Quixote,* Shakespeare's *Venus and Adonis,* or Zola's *Nana.* But a requirement that literature or art conform to some norm prescribed by an official smacks of an ideology foreign to our system." *Id.,* pp. 157–158.

In some States self-appointed groups either on their own or acting in concert with the police serve as unofficial censors in their effort to stop the distribution of literature deemed obnoxious. But since censorship is anathema to the First Amendment, the courts have been alert to enjoin those who threaten distributors with prosecution if they sell certain books, whether the censor be a self-appointed busybody or a police officer.

The dangers of censorship and prior restraint are the reasons why courts are wise in refusing to enjoin the publication of books or pamphlets that may, indeed, turn out to be defamatory and libelous. The point is illustrated by

Krebiozen Research Foundation v. *Beacon Press*, 134 N.E.
2d 1, decided by the Supreme Judicial Court of Massachusetts. The book sought to be enjoined was said to contain
wrongful and malicious statements about a drug which
plaintiffs sold and whose commercial value would be impaired by the book. The court, following *Near* v. *Minnesota*, refused to enjoin the distribution. ". . . full information and free discussion are important in the search for
wise decisions and best courses of action." *Id.*, p. 7. The
court conceded that this attack on the drug, if false, might
adversely affect its commercial value.

"But basing a rule on that possibility would end or at
least effectively emasculate discussion in the very controversial fields where it is most important. And it is hard
to believe that the publication of a critical book, even
though it contains false statements and is of false tenor
overall, will prevent the full testing of any substance
which in fact shows to the profession any promise of cur-
ing or alleviating cancer." *Id.*, p. 7.

An injunction against publication of the book would bar
the distribution of good and wholesome passages as well
as the false portions, for the tail must go with the hide. If
a judge could suppress all passages because he thought
some were false, he would be a censor. That would be let-
ting one man determine what should be read. Far better
that the book be published and the plaintiff sue for libel
and collect his damages than that a judge turn his talents
to censorship. In so deciding, the Massachusetts court spoke
in the great tradition of *Near* v. *Minnesota*.

71

The theatre and the movies differ from the press and the lecture platform only in form. The form, it is true, may make a vital difference in the impact of ideas conveyed. A play in cold print may be a lifeless thing. The human voice, gestures, facial expressions, body movements may bring it to life. A movie is more than the script. It is the harnessing of genius to awaken latent feelings, to challenge loyalties, to arouse prejudices, to instill courage or fear, and in a multitude of ways to arouse the emotions. A movie can carry an audience away more quickly than any orator. It has an impact in the raw that the other media usually lack.

These are the reasons usually advanced as grounds for censoring the theatre and particularly the movie. They are, I think, mistaken reasons. There is no room for censorship of any medium of expression in our society. Censorship is hostile to the First Amendment. That does not mean that the citizen can with impunity say what he likes, print what he likes, produce on the stage what he likes, draw or photograph what he likes for public showing. He is under restraints, as we have seen. But those restraints are carefully restricted and narrowly drawn to fit precise evils. They too operate as restraints in the manner in which all law tends to become a deterrent. But being narrowly drawn and being enforced by separate unrelated trials, they do not become a system whereby an individual, a board, or a committee subtly enforces its own moral, political, or literary code on the community. The Court has not gone so far as to strike down all censorship of the stage. It has been alert, however, to set aside orders of censors based on broad and inclusive powers.

Censorship assumes many forms. It has been a temptation for the Post Office to use the second-class mail privilege as an instrument to control the content of publications. This privilege is an extremely valuable one, being in substance a subsidy without which most magazines would be put out of business. Editors and publishers are extremely sensitive to the leverage that this privilege places in the hands of the Post Office. Unless restrained it could, indeed, become the power of life and death over a magazine. An Act of Congress states the conditions on which the privilege shall be granted: that the publication is "for the dissemination of information of a public character, or devoted to literature, the sciences, arts, or some special industry." The Post Office authorities ruled that this meant the magazine was "under a positive duty to contribute to the public good and the public welfare." *Hannegan* v. *Esquire*, 327 U.S. 146, 150. That ruling put the postal authorities in the seat of the censor, with the power of life or death over most magazines. The Court read the statute as granting no power of censorship. Whether a magazine meets the requirements of the statute is a decision that concerns primarily its format and whether its contents relate to "literature, the sciences, arts, or some special industry" —not "whether the contents meet some standard of the public good or welfare." *Id.*, p. 159.

Under other statutes the Post Office has undertaken vast powers of censorship. An Act of Congress, passed some eighty years ago when Grant was President, declares obscene publications "to be nonmailable matter and shall not be conveyed in the mails or delivered from any

73

post office or by any letter carrier." It also makes the mailing of such literature a crime. A system of extensive surveillance grew up under that law. Literature was barred from the mails on the ground that it was obscene without any notice or hearing. It took *Walker* v. *Popenoe*, 149 F. 2d 511, to impose the duty to give notice and provide a hearing before barring the mails to a publication.

In 1950, Congress passed a new postal obscenity law which gave the Post Office power to return all mail, stamped "unlawful," sent to anyone who was mailing obscene literature and bar payment of any money order to such person. The power was construed by the Post Office to give it authority to stop indefinitely all mail addressed to a person whom the department found to be trafficking in obscene publications, whether or not the particular mail was offensive. A stop order of that breadth was held unlawful in *Summerfield* v. *Sunshine Book Co.*, 221 F. 2d 42. The court held that stop orders of the Post Office "must be confined to materials already published, and duly found unlawful." *Id.*, p. 47. Were that not true, a vast, pernicious system of censorship would be fastened on the citizen. He would in effect be driven out of the publishing business for perhaps a single transgression; his legitimate activities, as well as the unlawful ones, would be stifled.

Mr. Justice Holmes said in his dissent in *Milwaukee Publishing Co.* v. *Burleson*, 255 U.S. 407, 437, "The United States may give up the Post Office when it sees fit, but while it carries it on the use of the mails is almost as much a part of free speech as the right to use our tongues. . . ." That is why Mr. Justice Holmes and Mr. Justice Brandeis dissented in *Leach* v. *Carlile*, 258 U.S. 138, 140–141, from a decision which sustained a statute allowing the Post Office to cut off the delivery of mail to a person adjudged by the department to be engaged in fraudulent use of the mail in selling commodities. They dissented because the Post Office order was a prior restraint operating against the sender of literature or letters.

Their view did not prevail and a system of prior restraint operates in full force in the fraud field. It likewise operates in the field of obscenity. It was suggested by way of dictum in *Near* v. *Minnesota*, 283 U.S. 697, 716, that prior restraint was permissible when dealing with obscenity. That would seem to be untenable, since all forms of censorship are in conflict with our constitutional system, for the reasons I have given. Certainly a system of censorship operating through the Post Office is as obnoxious as any other type of prior restraint, for as Mr. Justice Holmes said, "the use of the mails is almost as much a part of free speech as the right to use our tongues."

Licensing, one of the most notorious types of censorship, has been quite consistently struck down by the Court when applied to the distribution of literature. An ordinance requiring permission from the city manager to distribute literature in the city was held invalid on its face in *Lovell* v. *Griffin*, 303 U.S. 444. "Legislation of the type of the ordinance in question would restore the system of license and censorship in its baldest form," said Chief Justice Hughes. *Id.*, p. 452. The *Lovell* case has been closely followed. Its holding is essential to a free society, for its repudiation would mean that some official could determine what ideas could and what ideas could not be carried to the homes of the citizens. Obviously a newspaper or magazine need not get a license from the local or national government in order to publish. The printing and publishing business is not dependent on any bureaucrat's discretion for its existence. That freedom extends to all branches of the press—to the pamphleteer and to the door-to-door solicitor as well as to the more conventional printer or publisher.

The Court in *Thomas* v. *Collins*, 323 U.S. 516, 540, went much further and held that mere registration as a condition for making a public speech was not consistent with the First Amendment. Mr. Justice Rutledge wrote, "The restraint is not small when it is considered what was restrained. The right is a national right federally guaranteed. . . . If the restraint were smaller than it is, it is from petty tyrannies that large ones take root and grow." *Id.*, p. 543.

So far as I know, the only system of licensing of the press which we have today in America is the Act of July 29, 1954, by which Congress requires communist printing presses to be registered.

We have, of course, a system of licensing for radio and television stations. But the problem there is quite different. The channels all lie in the public domain, the air space above the earth being under the exclusive control of Congress. The channels are restricted in number. It is necessary to regulate all if interference is to be kept at a minimum and service is to be efficient. What the government owns or controls in the airways it can regulate as it sees fit. The licensing of radio and television stations is therefore not inconsistent with the requirements of the First Amendment. Those stations could not, of course, be turned over to the licensees as their private mouthpieces. They are public channels burdened with the duty of carrying all sides of public issues to the people.

Certainly, the government as licensor cannot by its regulations allow stations to disseminate only one set of ideas. The audience is entitled to a diversity and balance of views in the fields of public controversy. Government, having the management of the airways of the nation, must within feasible limits allow equal access by all groups. Any other course would be as acute abridgment of freedom of expression as barring the mails to all political parties but one.

The principle that forbids the exaction of a license for exercising a constitutional right also forbids taxing the privilege. *Murdock* v. *Pennsylvania,* 319 U.S. 105. "The power to tax the exercise of a privilege is the power to control or suppress its enjoyment." *Id.,* p. 112. If the contrary were true, the constitutional right would turn on the ability to pay. But financial considerations have no relevancy to First Amendment rights.

Printers and publishers must pay all the taxes that other citizens pay. The modern newspaper, for example, is in business for profit. There is no reason, therefore, why it should not share with the community the burden of all taxes which others pay. When, however, the press is singled out for special taxation, other considerations apply. The power to tax is the power to destroy, especially when it is exercised with a discriminating eye. Huey Long in his quest for political power in Louisiana singled out the opposition press for discriminatory treatment. The Court struck it down in *Grosjean* v. *American Press Co.*, 297 U.S. 233, analogizing it to the ancient and despised "taxes on knowledge."

IV. CONCLUSION

The First Amendment is not self-executing. It does not, for example, force open all avenues of knowledge. Although, in the philosophic sense, freedom of expression guarantees the right to know, express or implied prerogatives of government may close some channels and restrict others. It is the citizens' right to know that has been crucial in the struggle against secrecy in government. Yet secrecy in government is not fully eliminated by the First Amendment. The tendency of one administration to be close-mouthed about its executive and legislative activities may keep important information from the press. In recent years probably the greatest default has been the secrecy that has surrounded the nature and degree of radioactive fall-out from the explosions of the super-bombs. Our people have been constantly reassured and occasionally given limited information. But the necessary data for an informed public opinion on the subject have been withheld. One can get from novels like *On the Beach* by Nevil Shute a measure of the appalling and awful disaster that can befall humanity if a nuclear war comes. The recent book *Ra-*

diation by Schubert and Lapp reviews in sober language the alarming consequences of radiation through medical treatment, fall-out from bomb explosions, and the peaceful use of atomic energy. But the whole field has been veiled in such secrecy that only a partial account of radiation in the air we breathe, in the fields our cattle graze, in the reeds of the rivers that nourish marine life, in the plankton of the ocean on which our fish feed, has been made available to the public. Averages have sometimes been given; but the extent to which some areas have been seriously polluted has not been disclosed. Secrecy may be a necessary handmaiden of security to a degree. Yet no nation that faces unlimited destruction can afford to be uninformed.

"Naturally the first prerequisite for action and the constructive approach to the solution of a problem is knowledge. In this case we believe that awareness of the radiation hazard is most important. Intimate acquaintance with technical details of radiation problems is something better left to the expert. But because of official secrecy, it is often the case that 'outside experts' do not have full access to the facts. The only healthy way to evaluate the biological hazards of atomic energy and nuclear radiation is in the open air of public debate.

"Here the public can help by urging the government, through direct communication with elected representatives, that all information relating to nuclear-weapon effects be made available *promptly* to the nation's scientists." Schubert and Lapp, *Radiation* (1957), p. 255.

It was Patrick Henry who, during the debates preceding

79

adoption of the Constitution, spoke of the proper responsibility of government to inform its citizens:

"The liberties of a people never were, nor ever will be, secure, when the transactions of their rulers may be concealed from them. . . . I am not an advocate for divulging indiscriminately all the operations of government, though the practice of our ancestors, in some degree, justifies it. Such transactions as relate to military operations or affairs of great consequence, the immediate promulgation of which might defeat the interests of the community, I would not wish to be published, till the end which required their secrecy should have been effected. But to cover with the veil of secrecy the common routine of business, is an abomination in the eyes of every intelligent man. . . ."

But the responsibility of which Patrick Henry spoke cannot be insured by the judiciary. That even such a devout libertarian as Patrick Henry recognized a large legitimate area of government secrecy means that this responsibility must be enforced, if at all, through the executive and legislative branches, and through political action, a vigilant press, and an alert public opinion.

The problem of the right to know concerns foreign as well as domestic affairs. Yet when foreign affairs are concerned we confront special problems. Foreign policy is peculiarly in the keeping of the Executive. Yet, the policy of the government in refusing passports for travel to certain nations may in effect prevent the gathering of news that vitally affects the destiny and affairs of citizens of this country. That issue has been sharply posed in recent years by the mounting demand from the American press for permission to visit Red China and report to the American people the conditions that exist there. The Secretary of State defended the denial of passports to American reporters on several grounds, one being that they might not all be "responsible" journalists, another being that the "Constitutional freedom of the press relates to publication, not the gathering of news."

Dorothy Thompson, in reply, stated in the finest American tradition the function of the reporter:

"He does not exist to serve the Government but to inform the American people, and to do so with the utmost objectivity of which he is capable. The line he must hew to is the line of truth, and no other. If he is 'frivolous and irresponsible' [regarding the truth] he will be corrected by others. If his revelations do not support a Government policy, they may lead to a change in it. His value is that he is not the hired man of any government but a reporter and testifier of truth. He is 'responsible' exactly to the extent that he seeks to fulfill this function. And its fulfillment is not only his professional duty. It is his patriotic duty.

"The suggestion that freedom of reporting can exclude access to facts is extremely dangerous doctrine. The gleaning of facts is essential to knowledge, without which the right to publish is empty—and its exercise irresponsible.

"Dulles' concept of the function of the political re-

81

porter and analyst is close to that of all totalitarian states, and logically carried out in practice would lead to identical results."

The vice of secrecy in government has increased with the complexity of both domestic and foreign affairs and with the growth in the sheer size of government. As Wiggins in *Freedom or Secrecy* (1956), p. 225, says: "The trend toward secrecy in government, inspired by such fears and doubts about the safety with which information for the people can be given to the press, is pushing us farther and farther away from the concept of a free people that is the master and not the servant of its government."

There have been few exceptions to this tendency. The most outstanding are the Acts of May 29, 1957, passed by Connecticut, which give real substance to the right to know. One opens to the public all meetings (except executive sessions) of all agencies of the State and requires the votes of each member to be publicly recorded. The other opens to the public all records of all branches of government, unless the custodian concludes that disclosure would "adversely affect the public security or the financial interests" of government or that denial of access is "necessary to provide reasonable protection to the reputation or character of any person."

So much for the right to know. Now a final word as to freedom of expression.

Constitutional provisions sometimes have given little protection. This is particularly true where great numbers of the people have forgotten the values which those provisions are designed to protect and their leaders have failed to refresh their recollection. We have witnessed in this country a virtual witch hunt that has had a paralyzing effect on students, teachers, scientists, and writers. The unorthodox become suspect; the nonconformist is clouded with the same suspicions as the subversive. We have forced our scientists to live guarded lives. "The gossip of scientists who get together," Dr. J. Robert Oppenheimer once said, "is the lifeblood of physics." We have discouraged the gossip by confinement of our researchers to strictly orthodox channels. We have handicapped those who remained in the field, driven some like Oppenheimer and Edward Condon out, and discouraged young men from entering. There are other reasons also why we have lost ground in science, an area where we had long been out front. But this drive for orthodoxy is one of them.

During this period I visited Australia, a nation beset with many of the same perplexing problems of security as this country. Australia has no guarantee of freedom of expression in her written constitution. But her people have a profound respect for it in their hearts. The result was that during those tumultuous days Australia, without the written guarantee, showed far more respect for individual idiosyncrasies and diversity of views than we did in this country.

We were largely victims of the tyranny of a few who were beating the drums of fear. There is no protection against that tyranny which the law can provide. Charles W. Eliot of Harvard called it the pressure of "a concentrated multitudinous public opinion." In 1907, he showed how at times the pressure of public opinion was so great that a teacher had no alternative but silence or banishment. In other words, what we have witnessed during the last decade is not a new, but a recurring problem. Each generation must deal with it. The only protection is an enlightened public opinion forged by men who will stand against the mob. The antidote is more freedom of expression rather than less. The remedy is in making public opinion everybody's business and in encouraging debate and discourse on public issues. To regain the values "of the age of debate," as Dr. Hutchins put it, is one of the great problems of this generation.

To return to Pericles and his funeral oration, "We alone regard a man who takes no interest in public affairs, not as a harmless but as a useless character."

The Right
To Be Let Alone

I. THE RIGHT OF PRIVACY

Government exists for man, not man for government. The aim of government is security for the individual and freedom for the development of his talents. The individual needs protection from government itself—from the executive branch, from the legislative branch, and even from the tyranny of judges. The Framers of the Constitution realized this and undertook to establish safeguards and guarantees. Some of these concern the procedure that must be followed if government undertakes to move against the citizen. Others concern substantive rights such as freedom of religion and freedom of assembly.

There is, indeed, a congeries of these rights that may conveniently be called the right to be let alone. They concern the right of privacy—sometimes explicit and sometimes implicit in the Constitution. This right of privacy protects freedom of religion and freedom of conscience. It protects the privacy of the home and the dignity of the individual. Under modern conditions, it involves wiretapping and the use of electronic devices to pick up the confidences of private conversations. It also concerns the prob-

87

lem of the captive audience presented in *Public Utilities Commission* v. *Pollak,* 343 U.S. 451, where the Court held that streetcars could play radio programs to their captive audiences and that the passenger, no matter how offended he might be by the program, could only sit and listen—or walk to work.

I should also mention the right to travel—a right that today lies in the vague penumbra of the law because the final word has not yet been written. The Court has shown intolerance toward state restrictions against the free movement of people within the nation. *Edwards* v. *California,* 314 U.S. 160. But whether the government may prevent a citizen from traveling abroad because, for example, he has unpopular political beliefs is a phase of the problem yet unresolved.

This right to be let alone is a guarantee that draws substance from several provisions of the Constitution, including the First, the Fourth, and the Fifth Amendments. It was described in comprehensive terms by Mr. Justice Brandeis in his dissent in *Olmstead* v. *United States,* 277 U.S. 438, 478:

"The makers of our Constitution undertook to secure conditions favorable to the pursuit of happiness. They recognized the significance of man's spiritual nature, of his feelings and of his intellect. They knew that only a part of the pain, pleasure and satisfactions of life are to be found in material things. They sought to protect Americans in their beliefs, their thoughts, their emotions and their sensations. They conferred, as against the Government, the right to be let alone—the most comprehensive of rights and the right most valued by civilized men."

We often boast of our advance over the totalitarian regimes. We have tremendous advantages that they do not enjoy. Those advantages are not in material things such as technology and standards of living. They relate to matters of the mind and the spirit. They relate to the inalienable rights of man proudly proclaimed in our Declaration of Independence, and in part engrossed in our Constitution. Some call them legal rights; some natural rights. Natural rights were often invoked by the *laissez-faire* theorists of the late nineteenth and twentieth centuries to protect the nation's economy against governmental control. Conspicuous is the case of *Lochner* v. *New York*, 198 U.S. 45, holding unconstitutional a New York law setting ten hours as the work day of bakery employees, a decision that led Mr. Justice Holmes to say in dissent, "The Fourteenth Amendment does not enact Mr. Herbert Spencer's Social Statics." *Id.*, p. 75.

The natural rights of which I speak are different. They have a broad base in morality and religion to protect man, his individuality, and his conscience against direct and indirect interference by government. Some are written explicitly into the Constitution. Others are to be implied. The penumbra of the Bill of Rights reflects human rights which, though not explicit, are implied from the very nature of man as a child of God. These human rights were the products both of political thinking and of moral and religious

89

influences. Man, as a citizen, had known oppressive laws from time out of mind and was in revolt. Man, as a child of God, insisted he was accountable not to the state but to his own conscience and to his God. Man's moral and spiritual appetite, as well as his political ideals, demanded that he have freedom. Liberty was to be the way of life—inalienable, and safe from intrusions by government. That, in short, was our beginning.

Much of this liberty of which we boast comes down to the right of privacy. It is reflected in the folklore, which goes back at least as far as Sir William Staunford, that "my house is to me as my castle." But this right of privacy extends to the right to be let alone in one's belief and in one's conscience, as well as in one's home.

This right—the right to be let alone—has suffered greatly in recent years. Dr. A. Powell Davies recently pointed out how far we have gone in investigating opinions and beliefs:

> "Whatever an individual has thought or done—or even *may* have thought or done—should be discovered, if possible, to determine whether it has—or conceivably might seem to have—some bearing upon that individual's reliability as a citizen of the United States. Let us admit it: we now have in this country a system of investigation similar to that of the communists. It is not as harsh—not in most respects—but it has the same objects and uses some of the same methods. To a communist society, such a system is appropriate: it protects communism. To a free society, it can never be appropriate: it does *not* protect freedom, it destroys it."

90

We have entered this forbidden field out of a legitimate concern for the problem of subversion. These days the problem of the subversive centers around communism. There can be no denying the fact that communism and the Communist Party present special problems. Some countries have dealt with it in a special way. Thus the Constitution of the Republic of Vietnam, adopted in 1956, provides: "All activities having as their object the direct or indirect propagation or establishment of Communism in whatever form shall be contrary to the principles embodied in the present Constitution." That provision in effect withdraws the protection of free speech and a free press from this area. We have no such constitutional provision. Our theory from the beginning has been that our society is not so fragile that we must ban any discourse by any political party.

Yet the Communist Party is not just another political party. It is not indigenous to America; it has international connections and affiliations. Indeed, some legislatures have declared (and courts have sustained the finding) that the Communist Party of this country is part of an international conspiracy. Today the American Communist Party, following a change in its constitution, professes not to sanction the use of force and violence. But that profession is a recent one. Classically the Communist Party has advocated force and violence as political weapons.

These differences between the Communist Party and other political parties should not, however, blind us to four further considerations:

First, joining is an innate American habit. Men like Emerson fought it; but the habit grew and grew and became distinctly American. It is indeed the source of much of the power of self-help that appears and reappears in all phases of our life. This "passion for joining," as Professor Schlesinger once put it, has roots not only in our habits but in the First Amendment. Joining is one method of freedom of expression; it is a form of free inquiry; it is an exercise of the right of free assembly.

Second, for most of the years since World War I the Communist Party has been a wholly lawful party, not being outlawed by the States. In the election years from 1924 to 1940 it ran candidates for President; and one year it collected votes in thirty-seven States. As of 1955, the Communist Party was outlawed in only four States, all of those statutes being passed since 1950.

Third, guilt is personal under our system. A man can be punished for what he does, not for the acts of his friends, his associates, or his family. Joining the Communist Party does not necessarily indicate approval of all for which that organization stands, just as all who belong to the Presbyterian Church, the American Legion, or the American Bar Association do not necessarily endorse every tenet of those organizations. Prior to World War II, people joined the Communist Party for a number of reasons. As the Court recently said, speaking through Mr. Justice Black, in *Schware* v. *Board of Bar Examiners,* 353 U.S. 232, 245:

"During the depression when millions were unemployed and our economic system was paralyzed many turned to the Communist Party out of desperation or hope. It proposed a radical solution to the grave economic crisis. Later the rise of fascism as a menace to democracy spurred others who feared this form of tyranny to align with the Communist Party. After 1935, that Party advocated a 'Popular Front' of 'all democratic parties against fascism.' Its platform and slogans stressed full employment, racial equality and various other political and economic changes."

During that war, when Russia was our ally, many others joined the Communist Party. From reading many records in cases involving communists, I gather that many who joined may not have had subversion as a purpose. Some seemed to be sheer sentimentalists; others seemed utterly confused. Yet there has been a readiness to identify all who joined the party at any period of its existence with all of the aims espoused by it. That is guilt by association—a concept which is foreign to our history.

Fourth, is the command of the First Amendment which decrees that government has no concern with thoughts and beliefs. The search for political heresy which the threat of communism has engendered too readily identifies all unorthodox thought and expression as communistic. We have been too willing to sacrifice the rights of the unorthodox thinker to the search for communists. We have been too quick to identify someone who supports any portion of the party line—from political ownership of the means of production to equal rights for Negroes—as a communist. In short, the fear of communism has created an atmosphere which is antagonistic to a climate of tolerance for unortho-

93

dox thought and free communication of ideas which is so vital to a democracy.

We have witnessed in recent years a search for subversives which has not conformed to these American precepts. We have looked not only for the active, dedicated communists but also for those who once were communists, for those who associated with communists or who had communist relatives, for those who had sympathy with some of the reforms which communists promoted, and even for those whose ideas were unorthodox.

This search for subversives, like the search for heretics in an earlier age, led to excesses. The abuses caused the late Albert Einstein to say in 1954:

"If I would be a young man again and had to decide how to make my living, I would not try to become a scientist or scholar or teacher. I would rather choose to be a plumber or a peddler in the hope to find that modest degree of independence still available under present circumstances."

II. LEGISLATIVE INVESTIGATIONS

In recent years the right to be let alone has been dramatically emphasized by the activities of legislative committees. These committees perform a very important function in our system. They gather facts concerning proposed or possible legislation; and they inquire into the operation of existing laws to see if those measures are being faithfully administered or are adequate for the evil at hand. These are their functions; and both are adjuncts—indispensable adjuncts—of the law-making power.

It was once suggested that Congress has an additional function as well, the "informing function." See *United States* v. *Rumely*, 345 U.S. 41, 43. The idea was borrowed from Woodrow Wilson, who stated in his *Congressional Government* (1885), p. 303, "The informing function of Congress should be preferred even to its legislative function." That phrase, torn from its context, suggests that the power of Congress to "inform" the nation is independent of its legislative function. It is clear that Wilson meant no such thing. He was pleading for the dissemination of information concerning the administration of the laws. For the next sentence reads, "The argument is not only that discussed and interrogated administration is the only pure and efficient administration, but more than that, that the only really self-governing people is that people which discusses and interrogates its administration." *Id.*, p. 303.

The power to investigate is limited to the legislative function. A unanimous Court agreed in 1881 that neither the Senate nor the House possesses "the general power of making inquiry into the private affairs of the citizen." *Kilbourn* v. *Thompson*, 103 U.S. 168, 190. Inquiry is also precluded where the matter investigated is one on which "no valid legislation" could be enacted. *Id.*, p. 195. These are among the "recognized limitations" on "the power to investigate," as the Court said in the recent case of *Quinn*

v. *United States,* 349 U.S. 155, 161. The power is, in other words, merely an adjunct of the legislative power. Since Congress may not legislate on religion, it may not examine into religious beliefs. Since Congress may not establish a censorship over the press, it may not conduct an investigation which has that as an object.

This problem has been stirred on numerous occasions in our history. In 1832 John Quincy Adams, when he was in Congress, criticized a resolution that authorized an investigation of the United States Bank:

> "The subscriber believed that the authority of the committee and of the House itself did not extend, under color of examining into the books and proceedings of the bank, to scrutinize, for animadversion or censure, the religious or political opinions even of the president and directors of the bank, nor their domestic or family concerns, nor their private lives or characters, nor their moral, or political, or pecuniary standing in society. . . ."

There is a further requirement. Not only must the congressional committee's investigations be directed to a subject within the competence of the legislative function, but, before a witness may be punished in the courts for contempt of Congress, the particular questions which the witness refused to answer must be shown to be "pertinent" to the legitimate question under inquiry. The requirement of "pertinency" is an important protection, as the Court recently emphasized in *Watkins* v. *United States,* 354 U.S. 178. The investigating committee cannot, under the guise of a valid legislative inquiry, range broadly into a forbidden field.

There is another reason why Congress may not conduct certain types of investigations. As Chief Justice Warren said for the Court in *Quinn* v. *United States,* 349 U.S. 155, 161, the power to investigate does not include "any of the powers of law enforcement; those powers are assigned under our Constitution to the Executive and the Judiciary."

The Constitution expressly sanctions one type of legislative trial—the impeachment of public officials. And it expressly outlaws another type of legislative trial, known historically as a bill of attainder and so named in the Constitution. A bill of attainder is a resolution of the legislature which condemns a certain man or group of people and imposes a penalty. A bill of attainder is "a legislative act which inflicts punishment without a judicial trial." *Cummings* v. *Missouri,* 4 Wall. 277, 323. The punishment may be a fine, a jail sentence, or the confiscation of a man's property. If the legislature undertakes to bar a man from his profession or to provide that hereafter no funds shall be used to pay for his services, that too is a bill of attainder. *United States* v. *Lovett,* 328 U.S. 303.

A legislative committee may conduct another type of legislative trial. Without any legislative aim, it may turn its spotlight on an individual merely to destroy him for political or other reasons. That would also seem to be a legislative trial that is barred by the Constitution.

The idea of exposure by an investigating committee merely for exposure's sake, or to drive the citizen out of a job and into oblivion, or to bring the wrath of the com-

97

munity on to his head is foreign to our system. As the Court, speaking through Mr. Justice Black, said in *United States* v. *Lovett,* 328 U.S. 303, 318, "When our Constitution and Bill of Rights were written, our ancestors had ample reason to know that legislative trials and punishment were too dangerous to liberty to exist in the nation of free men they envisioned." And again, "They intended to safeguard the people of this country from punishment without trial by duly constituted courts." *Id.,* p. 317.

The distinction between a legislative investigation to determine what laws should be enacted and a legislative trial of a citizen is easy to state but difficult in practice to determine. Professor Edward L. Barrett, Jr., of the University of California, however, has maintained that the Tenney Committee, operating in California in the decade of the 1940's, usurped to itself functions of the executive and the judiciary in an attempt to corral subversives:

"Not content with mere exposure the committee sought to punish alleged subversives and their sympathizers, taking upon itself the functions of prosecutor, judge and jury. Once it had established to its satisfaction that a particular individual was a Communist or fellow traveler it sought literally to banish him from all normal community life. The objective was to quarantine him as though he were infected with smallpox. Efforts were made to prevent association with him, to forbid lawyers defending him in his troubles with the law, to cause his employer to discharge him and his union to expel him. People were warned that they should not rent him a hall for a meeting, or join any organization of which he was a member, or read any book or attend any play or motion picture written by him, or even espouse any cause espoused by him."

The best protection of the citizen against such a legislative trial is, of course, in the common sense and good judgment of the committee chairman. Legal restraints are important as well—particularly when Congress invokes the aid of the courts to punish the recalcitrant witness for contempt of Congress. When a witness refuses to answer questions, Congress has the power to compel his testimony by ordering that he be imprisoned until he answers or, at the latest, until the end of the session. *Anderson* v. *Dunn,* 6 Wheat. 204, 231. This is a power which Congress has not exercised in recent years. Rather, the practice has been to institute proceedings in the courts to punish a recalcitrant witness for contempt of Congress. As in other criminal cases, the courts have insisted that all elements of the crime be proved. Specifically, in these prosecutions, the courts must determine whether the congressional committee was pursuing an inquiry within the legislative competence, whether the questions asked the witness were pertinent to that inquiry, and whether the relevance of the question was made sufficiently clear to the witness. The task is often a difficult one.

It has been made still more difficult by the extremely broad resolutions by which both Houses of Congress have authorized certain of their committees to conduct investigations. For example, the resolution of the House of Rep-

99

resentatives authorized its Committee on Un-American Activities to investigate "un-American" propaganda and activities and "all other questions in relation thereto." Under that vague resolution the Committee since 1938 ranged broadly into many aspects of community life, including the investigation of magazines, newspapers, and all varieties of organizations. The vice of that broadly worded, vague resolution was stated for the Court by Mr. Chief Justice Warren in *Watkins* v. *United States*, 354 U.S. 178, 205.

"An excessively broad charter, like that of the House Un-American Activities Committee, places the courts in an untenable position if they are to strike a balance between the public need for a particular interrogation and the right of citizens to carry on their affairs free from unnecessary governmental interference. It is impossible in such a situation to ascertain whether any legislative purpose justifies the disclosures sought and, if so, the importance of that information to the Congress in furtherance of its legislative function. The reason no court can make this critical judgment is that the House of Representatives itself has never made it. Only the legislative assembly initiating an investigation can assay the relative necessity of specific disclosures.

"Absence of the qualitative consideration of petitioner's questioning by the House of Representatives aggravates a serious problem, revealed in this case, in the relationship of congressional investigating committees and the witnesses who appear before them. Plainly these committees are restricted to the missions delegated to them, i.e., to acquire certain data to be used by the House or the Senate in coping with a problem that falls within its legislative sphere. No witness can be compelled to make disclosures on matters outside that area. This is a jurisdictional concept of pertinency drawn from the nature of a congressional committee's source of authority. It is not wholly different from nor unrelated to the element of pertinency embodied in the criminal statute under which petitioner was prosecuted. When the definition of jurisdictional pertinency is as uncertain and wavering as in the case of the Un-American Activities Committee, it becomes extremely difficult for the Committee to limit its inquiries to statutory pertinency."

The vagueness of the resolution also presents a problem of serious proportions to the witness called before the Committee. Thus Watkins agreed to answer any questions about himself and any questions about present members of the Communist Party. He refused, however, to answer questions about people who once were, but no longer are, members.

"Having exhausted the several possible indicia of the 'question under inquiry,' we remain unenlightened as to the subject to which the questions asked petitioner were pertinent. Certainly, if the point is that obscure after trial and appeal, it was not adequately revealed to petitioner when he had to decide at his peril whether or not to answer. Fundamental fairness demands that no witness be compelled to make such a determination with so little guidance." *Id.*, p. 214.

The procedural requirement which the Court imposed in the *Watkins* case is one designed to protect the witness' right to be let alone—to insure to the witness his right to remain silent in response to an inquiry outside the legislative competence.

"Unless the subject matter has been made to appear with indisputable clarity, it is the duty of the investigative body, upon objection of the witness on grounds of pertinency, to state for the record the subject under inquiry at that time and the manner in which the propounded questions are propounded thereto. To be meaningful, the explanation must describe what the topic under inquiry is and the connective reasoning whereby the precise questions asked relate to it." *Id.*, p. 214.

The *Watkins* case also casts light upon another important restraint upon the power of legislative investigation—that imposed by the First Amendment.

The Court held in *West Virginia State Board* v. *Barnette*, 319 U.S. 624, that it was unconstitutional for a State to force students to salute the flag who had religious scruples against the act. The flag salute is a form of utterance that requires the declaration of a belief. If that belief collides with the religious principles of the students, it transgresses the command of the First Amendment that government shall make no law prohibiting "the free exercise" of a person's religion. The Court, speaking through Mr. Justice

Jackson, said, "If there is any fixed star in our constitutional constellation, it is that no official, high or petty, can describe what shall be orthodox in politics, nationalism, religion, or other matters of opinion or force citizens to confess by word or act their faith therein." *Id.*, p. 642. The Court went on to say that "the sphere of intellect and spirit" is protected by the First Amendment "from all official control." *Id.*, p. 642.

It is no longer open to doubt that the First Amendment protects freedoms of speech, press, and assembly, not only when legislatures enact laws which abridge those rights, but also when legislative committees conduct investigations abridging those freedoms. The Court, speaking through Mr. Chief Justice Warren, said in *Watkins* v. *United States*, 354 U.S. 178, 197:

> "Clearly, an investigation is subject to the command that the Congress shall make no law abridging freedom of speech or press or assembly. While it is true that there is no statute to be reviewed, and that an investigation is not a law, nevertheless an investigation is part of law-making. It is justified solely as an adjunct to the legislative process. The First Amendment may be invoked against infringement of the protected freedoms by law or by law-making.

> "Abuses of the investigative process may imperceptibly lead to abridgment of protected freedoms. The mere summoning of a witness and compelling him to testify, against his will, about his beliefs, expressions or associations is a measure of governmental interference.

And when those forced revelations concern matters that are unorthodox, unpopular, or even hateful to the general public, the reaction in the life of the witness may be disastrous. This effect is even more harsh when it is past beliefs, expressions or associations that are disclosed and judged by current standards rather than those contemporary with the matters exposed. Nor does the witness alone suffer the consequences. Those who are identified by witnesses and thereby placed in the same glare of publicity are equally subject to public stigma, scorn and obloquy. Beyond that, there is the more subtle and immeasurable effect upon those who tend to adhere to the most orthodox and uncontroversial views and associations in order to avoid a similar fate at some future time. That this impact is partly the result of non-governmental activity by private persons cannot relieve the investigators of their responsibility for initiating the reaction."

It would seem, therefore, that no investigating committee would be empowered to examine a pastor or priest on the tenets of his church.

By the same token a committee could not compel a witness to explain his tastes in art and literature, his musical preferences, his bent in science, his belief in evolution, or the way he reconciles it with the book of Genesis.

By the same token a committee could not compel an author to explain or justify the theses he supports in his writings nor defend his view against those of his contemporaries.

A committee could not force newspaper editors to explain or justify their editorial policies. That would amount to harassment for political, social, or economic views, which the First Amendment places beyond the power of government.

A minority report in 1953 of a committee of the American Society of Newspaper Editors, dealing with a legislative investigation of a newspaper editor, states, I think, the true American philosophy. The minority members emphasized that frequent and repeated congressional investigation of this kind "would extinguish, without the passage of a single law, that free and unfettered reporting of events and comment thereon, upon which the preservation of our liberties depends. . . ." They went on to say:

"A press that is under the continuing necessity of accounting to government for its opinions is not a free press —whether the government be a good or bad government. A press put to the frequent necessity of explaining its news and editorial policies to a United States Senator, armed with the full powers of the government of the United States, is not a free press—whether the Senator be a good or a bad Senator.

". . . If the spectacle of such an ordeal raises in the mind of the most timid editorial spectator an apprehension, a fear, a doubt and anxiety as to the safety with which he may report and as to the immunity with which he may legally comment, American freedom to that degree has suffered an impairment."

An investigation of the editorial page of a newspaper is kin to the kind of harassment that would result if a committee could subpoena and examine the subscribers to the newspaper to determine why they subscribed to that paper. Indeed, if the government could examine newspaper subscribers or purchasers of books, they could throw the shadow of the fear of retaliation over every subscription list. How many would be so bold as to read what they liked, if they ran the risk of being exposed by a congressional committee for their literary or political tastes?

Teaching in a classroom is certainly as much entitled to First Amendment protection as lecturing from a platform. It is the pursuit of truth which the First Amendment was designed to protect, no matter the method pursued. No method is more vital to our democracy than the classroom. For it nourishes our entire system, giving each generation of citizens the awareness of problems and the ingenuity for their solution. The philosophy of the *Barnette* case is that neither the lecturer nor the teacher can be compelled by the government to explain his philosophical, sociological, economic, religious, or political views. That is true both of public and private schools.

So far as the Constitution goes, private schools can, of course, discipline their faculty members and lecturers as they like. The First Amendment safeguards the citizen only against governmental action. Yet when private schools or universities discipline their faculty members or lecturers for their views on public issues, they may violate the democratic ideal. George Washington University recently announced that atheists had no place on its teaching and research staff, that it was limiting its faculty to believers in God. The reply of Dr. A. Powell Davies to the announcement of that policy reflects the true philosophy of the First Amendment. Freedom of discussion, he maintained, is available to atheists as well as to theists. If a minister fails to defend the role of an atheist to teach in a university, "he is denying the self-same principle upon which his own freedom is based every time he preaches from his pulpit." And in more philosophical terms he added, "What kind of God could He be who needed security measures to protect Him? . . . It is apostasy—all of it. And in a very deep sense, blasphemy. For God *lives* in the open mind, in the power of its thought, the voice of its truth, the inner impulse of its honesty. No shelter. No defenses. He needs no protection. Just give Him room." Religious tests have no place on the campus, he stated, adding that every university should have at least one or two atheists on its staff, "if only to keep the theists stepping lively."

Academic freedom in both private and state institutions is protected against encroachment by any arm of government. If it were otherwise, government, acting through investigative committees, could throw a shadow over every classroom in the land. By instilling the fear of investigation, it could put a real damper on academic freedom. Teachers or lecturers who might have to account to a committee tomorrow for the views they expressed today would tend to become timid, cautious souls. In practical effect the threat of any investigation of the classroom might serve as an effective prior restraint. He who questions the need to put the classroom under First Amendment protection should visit the universities of Russia, where the vigilant eye of the party member instantly detects every ideological stray. A visit to Russia is not essential for this lesson. A reading of *The Fall of a Titan* by Igor Gouzenko should be sufficient.

There can be no doubt that the national and state governments can take steps through investigation and otherwise to deal with the problems of subversion. As self-preservation is one aim of government, investigation to determine whether survival is threatened is proper. But, as I have said, those investigations reach a forbidden area when they touch on political beliefs. Overt acts have no immunity under the Constitution. The First Amendment, however, screens from the searching eyes of government a person's political beliefs. It's none of government's business whether a person rests the salvation of society on the single tax, socialism, the rule of the proletariat, or *laissez faire*. It's none of government's business what a farmer thinks of foreign policy, or what his attitude toward socialism is. The same is true of businessmen, plumbers, engineers, the whole range of the professions, and labor too. What the private citizen thinks or speaks or writes that prefers one political philosophy over another is under the protection of the First Amendment and immune from governmental surveillance.

An author or editor may not be compelled to testify as to why he favors or opposes socialized medicine, public power, equal rights for women, segregation of the races, or government by the proletariat. A teacher may prove his incompetence for the job by teaching socialism in the physics class or by using the course on labor relations to indoctrinate his students with dialectical materialism. Those acts may justify his discharge for abusing academic freedom. His convictions about socialism or dialectical materialism, however, are in the keeping of his conscience. Academic freedom protects thoughts, utterances, and beliefs. But it does not protect a violation of academic ethics nor put a wall of immunity around incompetence.

There is a wide spectrum by which loyalty is to be judged. Once aliens who refused to promise to take up arms on behalf of the United States were denied citizenship. But that rule was overturned by *Girouard* v. *United States*, 328 U.S. 61, which recognized that "even in time of war one may truly support and defend our institutions though he stops short of using weapons of war." *Id.*, p. 67. Loyalty is a broad banner under which many diverse groups may march. That is the philosophy of the First Amendment. That is, indeed, the secret of the powerful cohesive force that holds our nation together.

It was long assumed that communists were entitled to the same civil rights as other citizens. A 1937 decision rendered for the Court by Chief Justice Hughes in *De Jonge* v. *Oregon*, 299 U.S. 353, so ruled. That decision held that a State could not punish communists for holding a public meeting to discuss a matter of public concern. Chief Justice Hughes recognized that First Amendment rights might be abused "to incite to violence and crime." *Id.*, p. 364. But he added:

"The people through their legislatures may protect themselves against that abuse. But the legislative intervention can find constitutional justification only by deal-ing with the abuse. The rights themselves must not be curtailed. The greater the importance of safeguarding the community from incitements to the overthrow of our in-stitutions by force and violence, the more imperative is the need to preserve inviolate the constitutional rights of free speech, free press and free assembly in order to maintain the opportunity for free political discussion, to the end that government may be responsive to the will of the people and that changes, if desired, may be ob-tained by peaceful means. Therein lies the security of the Republic, the very foundation of constitutional gov-ernment." *Id.*, pp. 364–365.

Since those words were written, there has been a great change in attitude. Although, as I have said, communism presents special problems, we have indulged in many excesses concerning it. The regime of intolerance under which we have been living in recent years has deprived many men and women of their jobs, because they were or had been communists or were suspected of being such; and these jobs were ordinary jobs, not jobs in a sensitive area. Discharge for misconduct, inefficiency, unreliability, or a criminal record is one thing. Discharge for political belief is not the traditional Americanism of the First Amendment. Belief is entitled to refuge under the First Amendment where belief has not crossed the line into ac-tion, where belief has not been brigaded with conduct into a subversive scheme, where belief has not revealed traits inconsistent with the job. Freedom to believe has been conceived as absolute under the First Amendment, only action being subject to regulation in the public good.

Yet in recent years we have witnessed punishment for political heresy. One example is *Barsky* v. *Board of Regents*, 347 U.S. 442. That case sustained the suspension of a doctor from practice in New York for his failure to produce before a congressional committee certain papers that had been subpoenaed. He acted on advice of counsel, claiming that the committee acted unconstitutionally. There was no evidence of any kind that reflected on the doctor's professional ability. There was no evidence that he had done a single subversive act. There was no evidence that reflected on his character as a man or his record as a citizen. He had merely served as an officer of the Joint Anti-Fascist Refugee Committee which had opposed Franco in Spain and which was on the Attorney General's list of subversive organizations. The doctor was suspended because he was on the unpopular side of a controversial issue, not because he was incompetent as a doctor or disloyal as a citizen.

Matters of political or economic belief are supposed to be beyond the reach of government. One steeped in our history would never dream that a citizen could be denied the privilege of practicing law or medicine because of his views on foreign policy.

Two decisions that followed the *Barsky* case reflect a more tolerant attitude. In *Schware* v. *Board of Bar Examiners*, 353 U.S. 232, and *Konigsberg* v. *State Bar*, 353 U.S. 252, the Court held that membership in the Communist Party during the years before World War II did not, in and of itself, justify a State's refusal to allow an applicant to practice law. In holding that denial of the privilege of practicing law for that reason constituted a denial of due process, the Court, speaking through Mr. Justice Black in the *Schware* case, said:

"During the period when Schware was a member, the Communist Party was a lawful political party with candidates on the ballot in most States. There is nothing in the record that gives any indication that his association with that Party was anything more than a political faith in a political party. That faith may have been unorthodox. But as counsel for New Mexico said in his brief, 'Mere unorthodoxy [in the field of political and social ideas] does not, as a matter of fair and logical inference, negative good moral character.'" *Id.*, p. 244.

Unorthodoxy in the field of political and social ideas is no business of government. When government respects that principle, the right of the people to be let alone in their opinions and beliefs is secure.

I have already mentioned some of the problems which are engendered by vague, broad legislative resolutions which have been employed to justify sweeping investigations. An additional problem is created by these vague resolutions in relation to the right of silence guaranteed by the First Amendment. As noted, the Court dealt with that problem in *Watkins* v. *United States*, 354 U.S. 178. But the First Amendment problem was more clearly focused in *Sweezy* v. *New Hampshire*, 354 U.S. 234, decided the same day.

New Hampshire's legislature had empowered the New

Hampshire Attorney General to act as a one-man legislative committee to investigate the activities of "subversive persons." The Attorney General put questions to Paul Sweezy concerning the Progressive Party and the contents of a lecture on socialism that Sweezy had delivered to the students of a humanities course at the University of New Hampshire. Sweezy refused to answer on grounds that the questions were not pertinent to the matter under inquiry and infringed upon an area protected by the First Amendment. He was adjudged in contempt for his refusal to answer. His conviction was affirmed by the New Hampshire courts but reversed by the Supreme Court. The reversal was in my view justified on several grounds, *inter alia* because the questions he had refused to answer were in the areas of academic freedom and political expression.

In both the *Watkins* and *Sweezy* cases, the Court has been aligned, when dealing with the scope of the legislative investigating power, on the side of the right to be let alone.

III. LOYALTY INVESTIGATIONS

The extensive and intensive investigations of the loyalty of government employees, which we have experienced in recent years, have trenched heavily on the rights of citizens. I shall discuss only the federal programs of investigations. They cover, however, only a part of the field. The seriousness of the problem is shown by the fact that not only the state governments but business itself has entered this field. Whether a man works in a county courthouse or in an industrial plant his beliefs, as well as his past conduct, are being probed these days. Loyalty investigations are nationwide and reach all levels of employment.

On March 21, 1947, there was promulgated a comprehensive scheme for the removal of government employees from the payroll, if reasonable grounds existed for the belief that the employee was disloyal to the government of the United States. Under that order, grounds for dismissal ranged from sabotage to membership in organizations designated as subversive by the Attorney General, and the advocacy of revolution.

This procedure, utilized to brand government employees as disloyal, was a departure from traditional American concepts of fair play and due process of law. The employee brought before the Loyalty Board could be condemned on the basis of anonymous information contained in the Board's files. His accusers were not required to confront him. Therefore, no one knew whether the accuser was truthful or only getting even for an old grudge. The derogatory information might be no more than a crank letter or an indication that the employee had known at one time or another a subversive person. Judge Edgerton said, dissenting in *Bailey* v. *Richardson*, 182 F. 2d 46, 68, ". . . the minimum standards of fairness that are known as due process of law" include an opportunity to cross-examine the opposing witnesses. "Hardly any protection at all is possible against vague assertions of unseen and unknown persons." *Id.*, p. 68. Those who try and brand people as subversives on the basis of faceless informers engage in an un-American practice. Those who suffered from the practice and cried out against it were pleading for the traditional American standard of fair play.

The procedural unfairness in these trials of employees was summed up in *The Fear of Freedom,* by Francis Biddle. "It is an ironic and not altogether happy reflection that although Congress has written into the law the elementary requirements of fair procedure for the Government to follow in administrative hearings involving property rights, the same safeguards have been here denied to its own employees."

These excesses were highlighted by the 1957 report of the Commission on Government Security. The Commission recommended that persons subjected to loyalty investigations be given the right to cross-examine their accusers whenever that could be accomplished "without endangering the national security." The Commission's report acknowledged that the procedural rights of government employees had not been fully protected in the preceding ten years. "Those whose livelihood and reputation may be affected by such loyalty investigations are entitled to fair hearing and to decisions which are neither capricious nor arbitrary." *Id.*, p. xviii.

In 1951, the standard for dismissal was changed—an employee was to be dismissed, not if there was reasonable ground to believe him disloyal, but if a reasonable doubt as to his loyalty existed. Under this standard a government employee could be required to prove his loyalty beyond the shadow of a doubt or face discharge and an adjudication that he was disloyal to the United States.

Some insight into the way the system operated can be gained by a look at the case of John S. Service. In 1951, Service had been a Foreign Service officer for sixteen years, spending ten of those years in China. Before the loyalty program was established, Service had been cleared of charges of disloyalty in 1945, 1946, and 1947 by the State Department. In 1949, 1950, and 1951, the State Department's Loyalty Security Board determined that no reasonable grounds existed for a belief that Service was disloyal, and that there was no reasonable doubt as to Service's loyalty. But in December of 1951, the Civil Service Commission's Loyalty Review Board concluded a "post-audit" of Service's case (a procedure which the Court later held to be unauthorized in the case of *Peters* v. *Hobby*, 349 U.S. 331). The same day that the Loyalty Review Board decided on the same evidence that had previously been before the State Department Board, that there was a reasonable doubt as to Service's loyalty, Secretary of State Dean Acheson discharged him. This was in face of the record which showed that Service had been cleared six times. After five and one half long years, during which Service sought relief before administrative bodies and in the courts, the Court decided that Service's dismissal was invalid. Acheson had taken a short cut, and had acted in contravention of the State Department's own regulations when he discharged Service. *Service* v. *Dulles*, 354 U.S. 363.

A new security program was promulgated in 1953. Under the new regulations a suspected employee was immediately suspended by an officer, often one unknown to him and before whom he could not plead his case. Although his suspension was "in the interests of the national security," this suspension could be for a variety of reasons. It was not even necessary, as it was under the earlier program, that there be evidence of espionage, sedition, or affiliation with subversive groups. Under the 1953 security program, loyalty, security, and suitability were lumped together. The public, however, often assumed that any person who was accused, terminated, or resigned under this program had been disloyal to his country.

The evil of that system is shown in the case of Evelyn Burrell, an Army clerk-typist who was removed from her position in 1952 on loyalty grounds. Although she was cleared of those charges, in 1953 the Civil Service Commission found her unsuitable for federal employment because of alleged false statements concerning "material loyalty matters" at her hearing. After a "merry-go-round of litigation" lasting over three years, Judge Bazelon, speaking for the Court of Appeals of the District of Columbia, held the discharge unlawful. He referred to the "badge of infamy" which attaches to a finding of disloyalty. "Though appellant was ostensibly cleared on loyalty charges, the charges on which she was found unsuitable are of the same stuff and stain. The Commission's action kept the word of promise to the ear but broke it to the hope." *Burrell* v. *Martin*, 232 F. 2d 33, 40. The evil of blending trials for suitability with trials for loyalty was emphasized in the 1957 report of the Commission on Government Security. The Commission recommended that loyalty cases be separated from those involving suitability or security. "A man who talks too freely when in his cups, or a pervert who is vulnerable to blackmail, may both be security risks although both may be loyal Americans. The Commission recommends that as far as possible such cases be considered on a basis of suitability to safeguard the individual from an unjust stigma of disloyalty." *Id.*, p. xvii.

It was a brave employee who was willing to hire a lawyer and face the blast of publicity and the uncertainty of a hearing in which his accusers remained anonymous. Even if he won, he would not be automatically re-employed. Though he were able to prove his loyalty, honesty, integrity, and trustworthiness, he would not be reinstated unless the head of his agency found this "consistent with the interests of national security."

When policy-making jobs in the government are involved, there are situations where one's belief is relevant to the issue of his fitness for the particular job. One who is passionately dedicated to the defeat of all public power projects would not be the best person to manage a public power program. One who passionately believes in passive resistance and is opposed to war would not be the best person to manage the Selective Service System. One who is in favor of the dictatorship of the proletariat certainly should not administer our atomic research. And so on. But the fact that belief may be a disqualifying consideration does not warrant the government in issuing a decree or order branding a citizen as unfit, dangerous, or subversive.

The head of a department can select his employees as he chooses, shuffling and reshuffling the cards until he gets what by his lights is the best staff available. Once the staff is assembled and he has doubts as to either the capability or the trustworthiness of any employee, he can move him on to different work, less important work, or less sensitive work as he chooses. If there is even the faintest suspicion of his integrity, he can move him to work where policy is not made and where confidential files are not accessible or he can discharge him.

The loyalty program proceeded on no such basis. The loyalty program was in effect a trial of government employees ending in orders or decrees that an employee was or was not loyal to this nation, was or was not a person with subversive tendencies, was or was not a good security risk.

That was the central evil and vice of the loyalty program —a feature that the 1957 report of the Commission on Government Security accepts without question. A citizen who left the loyalty proceedings condemned as unfit for public service and unworthy of public trust was officially branded. That branding often led to ostracism and the end of a career to which he had given the best years of his life. The Court recognized this when, speaking through Mr. Justice Clark in *Wieman* v. *Updegraff*, 344 U.S. 183, 190–191, it said: "There can be no dispute about the consequences visited upon a person excluded from public employment on disloyalty grounds. In the view of the community, the stain is a deep one; indeed, it has become a badge of infamy." If the reason he was condemned was unlawful conduct, he should have been turned over to the prosecutor's office. He should not have been tried in administrative proceedings where he had none of the benefits of the Fifth and

Sixth Amendments, including trial by jury and the right to be confronted by his accusers.

If the reason he was condemned was his beliefs and opinions, then the government also transgressed the First Amendment. It is no answer to say, as Mr. Justice Holmes once did, that no one has the constitutional right to be a policeman or to do other work for the government. The Constitution contains no guarantee of employment in any field. But it does contain guarantees that government may not do certain things to the citizen. Foremost is the command of the First Amendment that government will make no law penalizing the citizen for his beliefs, his conscience, and his utterances. A loyalty order that casts a citizen into the outer darkness because of his speeches or beliefs does just that.

The Court has recognized the awful effect upon an employee of any order which adjudges that he is disloyal, or that his continued employment will adversely affect the national security. The fact that such a finding is "a badge of infamy" was emphasized by Chief Justice Warren in a leading case that construed the loyalty and security orders narrowly. *Peters* v. *Hobby,* 349 U.S. 331, 347. That is, indeed, the background against which the Court has limited the immense scope which administrative officials gave those orders. *Cole* v. *Young,* 351 U.S. 536. For, as the Court said, speaking through Mr. Justice Harlan, ". . . in view of the stigma attached to persons dismissed on loyalty grounds, the need for procedural safeguards seems even greater than in other cases, and we will not lightly assume that Congress intended to take away those safeguards in the absence of some overriding necessity, such as exists in the case of employees handling defense secrets." *Id.*, pp. 546–547.

To repeat, government need not sit supine and let subversives take it over or infiltrate it with spies. Men or women can be removed from sensitive jobs for good reasons or for no reasons at all. Employees can be reassigned or demoted or even dropped from the service. The evil which has arisen lies in the decree or order that publicly stigmatizes him by administrative decree for traitorous conduct or for dangerous thoughts or expressions. It is the business of government to punish people only if they have committed crimes and have been duly convicted in a judicial trial and pursuant to the requirements of due process of law.

I have already mentioned the special problems presented by communism. But the available statistics do not demonstrate that the loyalty and security programs have had a great deal of success in protecting our government from the dangers of communism or of subversion from within. The game does not seem to have been worth the candle. The available statistics do not show that any significant number of government employees were disloyal. We can be confident that the overwhelming percentage of condemned employees were outlawed not for crimes but for indiscretions, not for disloyal conduct but for unorthodox and unpopular speech and beliefs.

The effects on the government services have been devastating, especially in critical areas of policy formulation. Condemnation of public servants for their beliefs or expressions has the inevitable result of substituting pallid orthodoxy for the independence of thought, ingenuity, and boldness of decision which effective public service demands.

One example is in the field of foreign relations. Many of those who a decade ago saw a feudal leader as a bankrupt politician or a colonial power as a breeder of communism, and who felt that revolution was on its way, put their ideas in official memoranda to their superiors. Those men—at least many of them—have been hunted men. Though not communists, now or in the 1940's, they did not express their ideas in anti-communist terms. They have been ridden out of the service for their views. Their example has not gone unnoticed. These days it would take a bold man in the field, especially a junior, to espouse the cause of socialism—not as the political creed for America but as the best political antidote for communism in Asia. It would take a bold junior to oppose the *status quo* in a feudal nation for fear of being catalogued with the communists. It would take a courageous junior to support Nehru, when the Western world has been led to think that Nehru is a friend of communism.

There are bold juniors in our service. But they are not conspicuous. The truth is, I think, that the loyalty program has had a great leveling effect. Juniors abroad now tend to write safe memoranda to their seniors, for they remember their predecessors who were sacrificed for the expression of their unorthodox beliefs in the 1940's. Juniors abroad tend to conform their thinking to orthodox views, to venture no bold theory or course of action, to tender no imaginative concept for dealing with a dangerous situation.

The loyalty programs have, I fear, greatly crippled us by putting many of our employees abroad in fear of imaginative reporting. As a result, we are becoming more and more disadvantaged in dealing with the crises in the world. Plagued by the orthodoxy that loyalty proceedings have instilled, we go from crisis to crisis, never fully prepared for any of them and almost invariably surprised at the depth and power of the forces operating in each situation.

This was the situation which prompted Louis J. Halle, long in the service of the State Department, to write in November, 1954:

> "One hopes that the American public will see at last that the word 'security' has become a euphemism. It covers the primitive political drive of the last five years to eliminate intellectual and moral distinction from the Government service, and to staff the Government instead with political good fellows who cannot be suspected of superiority. Under the reorganized Foreign Service, for example, educational standards for admission are being avowedly lowered. It is as if the mediocrity of the mindless has become the ideal."

Certainly, the "mediocrity of the mindless" can be the only result of a system where unorthodox views and beliefs are suspect.

The loyalty programs for government employees have wrought great injustices to many of our citizens and have led the government to invade provinces which we thought were sacred from interference. The initial error from which all others flowed was in investigating attitudes and beliefs. In that field the Constitution said the citizen should be let alone. Yet it was in that field that government raised the most havoc and did the most damage. The moral is reflected in Justice Brandeis' dictum:

> "The greatest dangers to liberty lurk in insidious encroachment by men of zeal, well-meaning but without understanding." *Olmstead* v. *United States*, 277 U.S. 438, 479.

IV. THE DESPISED OATHS

Justice Black, in his dissent in *Communications Assn.* v. *Douds*, 339 U.S. 382, 448, spoke of test oaths as the "implacable foes of free thought." They have a long and controversial history. They were, indeed, oppressive to the consciences of men. They were instruments of tyranny when unorthodox beliefs were considered dangerous by the powers-that-be.

First, and most notorious, is the oath *ex officio*. The oath *ex officio* was introduced into the English ecclesiastical courts in the early part of the thirteenth century. This interrogatory oath, a significant departure from prior ecclesiastical procedure, required the accused to swear "to answer all such interrogatories as shall be offered to you and declare your whole knowledge therein, so God you help." The oath, especially when combined with procedures whereby the accused was not informed of the nature of the charges against him, and was not confronted by his anonymous accusers, was particularly suited to the trial of heresy and other crimes of conscience. It was a procedure used to open windows into a man's soul, to probe his mind by compelling him to answer questions concerning his beliefs.

In 1559, Elizabeth established a national church and required conformity from all her subjects. To ferret out religious nonconformity, she empowered the Court of High Commission to proceed *ex officio* in the trial of heresy. The Puritans recognized that it was the oath *ex officio* which constituted the crux of the High Commission's procedures to inquire into their thoughts and beliefs. They instituted a bitter fight against the oath. Here, they found allies in the common-law courts, led by Lord Coke, who maintained that the oath was illegal. By the early seventeenth century, the common-law courts had prevailed, issuing their writs to preclude the use of the *ex officio* oath by the High Commission.

The battle had not yet been won. The Star Chamber continued to use its vast jurisdiction to try political crimes and cases involving religious nonconformity. Following the ecclesiastical rules, the Star Chamber required the accused to take the oath *ex officio*. Opposition to the oppressive methods of the Star Chamber came to a head in the trial of John Lilburne before the Star Chamber. 3 How. St. Tr. 1315 (1637). Lilburne, charged with importing heretical and seditious books, refused to be examined under oath. He proclaimed to the judges of the Star Chamber, "this oath I refused as a sinful and unlawful oath." Lilburne advanced many arguments against the oath. One of his objections to it was that it invaded the sanctity of the conscience and violated the dignity of man. He told the judges:

> "as for that Oath that was put upon me, I did refuse to take it as a sinful and unlawful oath, and by the strength of my God enabling me, I will never take it, though I be pulled in pieces by wild horses, as the ancient Christians were by the bloody tyrants in the Primitive Church; neither shall I think that man a faithful subject of Christ's kingdom, that shall at any time hereafter take it, seeing the wickedness of it hath been so apparently laid open by so many, for the refusal whereof many do suffer cruel persecutions to this day." *Id.*, p. 1332.

Despite his spirited defense of his right to refuse the oath, Lilburne was convicted of contempt and sentenced to be whipped publicly and fined.

The Star Chamber's victory was to be short-lived. In 1641, the House of Commons ordered reparation to Lilburne, proclaiming that Lilburne's sentence was illegal and against the liberty of the subject. A few months later, Parliament abolished the Star Chamber and the *ex officio* oath.

The *ex officio* oath had only a short history in the American Colonies. The Massachusetts Body of Liberties of 1641 outlawed compulsory testimony by an accused, either by torture or under oath. There is some early history of the use of the oath *ex officio* in Virginia, but the oath was definitely abolished in that colony by 1661.

Yet the hated and despised oath *ex officio* lived on in the memory of man. The animosities generated by it made many other oaths unbearable.

Test oaths and loyalty oaths, apart from the oath *ex officio*, have a long history. In 1543, Henry VIII required all persons holding office under him or doing any fealty to him to swear to a complex oath renouncing the authority of the Bishop of Rome, and pledging continued allegiance to the king and his successors. Elizabeth, in 1558, required the clergy and all public officers to attest the Queen's spiritual and temporal sovereignty, and to renounce the pretended power of all foreign persons and states. Five years later, the number of persons required to take the oath was enlarged to include scholars, teachers, lawyers, and court officers. In 1593, Elizabeth required all her subjects to attend Anglican church services. Those who failed to attend, or who held nonconformist religious meetings, were forced to confess their offense against God, and to swear to attend the Anglican services.

James I required those who showed signs of religious nonconformity to take a comprehensive oath, renouncing the authority of the Pope over the king and the king's subjects, and promising to disclose to the king all "traitorous conspiracies." Later, the oath was required generally of all persons above the age of eighteen, and specifically of clerics, nobles, lawyers, physicians, public officials, teachers, and scholars. The oath, as well as the sacrament of

127

the last supper, was made prerequisite to naturalization.

As opposition to the taking of such oaths mounted, Charles II made it unlawful to advocate that the taking of a required oath is unlawful. In the same year, 1662, Charles II required an oath of the clergy and the teaching profession to conform to the liturgy of the Anglican church and to abandon attempts to change the government of church or state. In 1672, Charles II required all public officers to take the same oath that had been required by James I sixty-seven years earlier. And, in addition, he required a renunciation of belief in the Catholic doctrine that transubstantiation of bread and wine into the body and blood of Christ occurs during the sacrament of the Lord's supper. And, in 1677, members of Parliament, to be eligible to vote or even to sit during debate, were required to take an oath renouncing the religious doctrines of the Catholic church.

The Puritans, who fled religious persecution in England, were required to take the oaths attesting the supremacy of and allegiance to the English sovereign before boarding ship. Once at sea, they were required to say Anglican prayers.

Loyalty oaths appeared in this country during the Civil War. In the North, persons jailed for disloyalty could obtain their freedom only by taking an oath swearing loyalty to the Union cause. Hyman, *Era of the Oath*, 34 (1954). As the Northern armies advanced into the South, Union commanders required the civilian populace to swear loyalty to the Union. In 1862, Congress required an iron-clad oath of past, present, and future loyalty of all elected and appointed employees of the government, excepting only the President of the United States—an Act which continued in effect until 1884. Those unwilling to swear that they had not aided, countenanced, counseled, or encouraged armed hostility against the United States were made ineligible for public office or employment. Congress required all jurors in the federal courts to take an oath that they had not adhered to or given assistance to a rebellion against the United States.

The congressional oath of 1862 was extended to all attorneys who wished to practice before the federal courts. It was this oath which was held unconstitutional in *Ex parte Garland*, 4 Wall. 333. The State of Missouri required, in its 1865 Constitution, that voters, public employees, jurors, attorneys, corporate officers, teachers, and clergymen execute an oath that they had not, by word or deed, aided the rebel cause. It was this oath that was held unconstitutional in *Cummings* v. *Missouri*, 4 Wall. 277.

Today, more loyalty oaths are required to be executed in the United States than at any time in our history. Labor unions are not entitled to the benefits of the National Labor Relations Act unless union officers execute an affidavit that they are not members of an organization which believes in or teaches overthrow of government by illegal means. This was the oath sustained in *Communications Assn.* v. *Douds*, 339 U.S. 382.

Many of the States require oaths of past, present, or future loyalty, or any combination of these three, as a condition of public employment. In these States, all persons on the public payroll are required to execute a loyalty oath including, indiscriminately, janitors, bookkeepers, school-teachers, and professors in state colleges. Loyalty oaths have been specifically required for non-academic employees of state universities, for schoolteachers in the public schools, for tenants in public housing projects, and even for those who claim exemption from certain state taxes.

An oath requiring a pledge of present loyalty to the government by a person taking public office or seeking it is certainly unobjectionable. He who enters a public office does so as trustee for the people. It is not too much to demand that he pledge in the most solemn manner possible his dedication to the principles of our government, which, of course, allow for change—even radical change—but do not sanction the use of force to accomplish that change or to destroy our institutions. That is the force of the ruling in *Gerende* v. *Election Board*, 341 U.S. 56, which sustained a state law requiring a person who desires a place on the ballot to take an oath that he is not engaged in any attempt to overthrow the government by force and violence nor a knowing member of an organization engaged in such an attempt.

The other oaths with which the courts have dealt have had greater complexities. The *Cummings* and the *Garland* cases mark some of them.

In those cases persons holding offices of trust were required to take an oath (in the *Cummings* case a state oath, in the *Garland* case a federal oath) that they had not in any way favored the South against the North or adhered to the enemies of the North. Cummings was a Catholic priest who was convicted by the Missouri courts for teaching and preaching without having first taken the oath. Garland was a lawyer who, though pardoned by the President, could not take the federal oath, necessary for members of the Bar of the Supreme Court, because he had been a member of the Congress of the Confederacy.

These oaths had no relation to the fitness of the priest or the lawyer respectively for the professions they sought to follow. As the Court said in the *Cummings* case, the oath was required "in order to reach the person, not the calling. It was exacted, not from any notion that the several acts designated indicated unfitness for the callings, but because it was thought that the several acts deserved punishment, and that for many of them there was no way to inflict punishment except by depriving the parties, who had committed them, of some of the rights and privileges of the citizen." 4 Wall. 320.

The exaction of the oath was punishment since it outlawed whole classes from employment. "To them there is no escape provided; to them the deprivation was intended to be, and is, absolute and perpetual. To make the enjoyment of a right dependent upon an impossible condition is equivalent to an absolute denial of the right under any condition, and such denial, enforced for a past act, is nothing less than punishment imposed for that act." *Id.*, p. 327.

To deprive a man of his calling or his profession may be more severe than to impose on him a fine or a prison term. The right to work may be as precious a type of "liberty" as any that is guaranteed by the Fifth and Fourteenth Amendments.

The Framers of the Constitution dealt pervasively with

punishment and indicated how it could and could not be imposed. Two methods outlawed, both to the States and to the Congress, were bills of attainder and *ex post facto* laws. These expurgatory oaths were bills of attainder because they were in substance forms of punishment imposed by the legislatures for past conduct. The Constitution outlaws deprivation of liberty "for past conduct by legislative enactment, under any form, however disguised." *Id.*, p. 325. These expurgatory oaths were also *ex post facto* laws since they imposed punishment for an act that was not punishable when it was committed, or added retroactively additional punishments.

It is difficult to reconcile *Garner* v. *Los Angeles Board*, 341 U.S. 716, decided in 1951, with the philosophy of the *Cummings* and *Garland* cases. A condition of employment in the City of Los Angeles was an oath that the applicant had not advocated the overthrow of the governments of the United States or of California by force and violence or been a *knowing* member of a group that so advocated. A divided Court sustained the exaction of the oath as a reasonable qualification for a city post. To uphold the oath is to make that membership—both past and present—an absolute bar to city employment.

As Mr. Justice Burton said in dissent, "It leaves no room for a change of heart. It calls for more than a profession of present loyalty or promise of future attachment. It is not limited in retrospect to any period measured by reasonable relation to the present. In time this ordinance will amount to the requirement of an oath that the affiant has *never* done any of the proscribed acts." *Id.*, p. 729.

The result is that the applicant was barred from showing a repentance for past misdeeds and present fitness for a job demanding loyalty. *Garner* sustained legislative punishment of those who once erred where *Cummings* and *Garland* denounced it. *Garner* took past advocacy of a subversive creed as an absolute test of loyalty, disregarding the doctrine of redemption and forgiveness so deep in our customs.

Wieman v. *Updegraff*, 344 U.S. 183, is in a better tradition. Oklahoma passed a law which required each state officer or employee to take an oath that he was not, and had not been for the past five years, a member of any communist front or subversive organization so classified by the Attorney General of the United States. The Court, speaking through Mr. Justice Clark, held that the oath violated the requirement of due process since it penalized membership in the proscribed organizations that was innocent as well as that which was informed and knowing. "Indiscriminate classification of innocent with knowing activity must fall as an assertion of arbitrary power." *Id.*, p. 191.

Plainly the punishment for a past innocent act was a bill of attainder, as the *Cummings* and *Garland* cases teach. But the vice of the oath in *Wieman* v. *Updegraff* struck deeper.

As I have said, joining is an innate American habit. It is a method of expression—an assertion of First Amendment rights. One joins to identify himself with certain objects of the group or to find a hospitable climate of opinion for the pursuit of ideas. One may join a group to associate himself with laudable and lawful aims of the organization,

133

not knowing that a small group in control has a secret, sinister objective. If a person is to be deprived of his livelihood because of any association, no matter how innocent, with a subversive group, then a great damper is placed on the free pursuit of knowledge.

One who fears retaliation for associating with groups, seemingly innocent and lawful, will confine himself to more orthodox activities. Under that climate of opinion the free spirit so necessary for research and teaching is greatly limited. That problem was central in the *Wieman* case, since the employees in question were members of the faculty of the Oklahoma Agricultural and Mechanical College. *Wieman* v. *Updegraff* is, therefore, a milestone in academic freedom.

One great right protected by the First Amendment is the right of silence. It has its roots in the opposition to the oath *ex officio* and to the other oaths exacted from the citizen in early English history. Much of that history has been forgotten in recent years as our search for the modern heretic has gone forward. We have drifted more and more to penalizing belief and punishing those who will not expose their beliefs. It is the overt act, not political belief or advocacy, that should be the crime or the reason for inflicting the penalty. Only when we return to that standard will we truly respect the right of silence inherent in the First Amendment.

As I have said, communism presents special problems. But the exaction of loyalty oaths from tenants in public housing projects and from churches that seek tax exemptions shows the extreme to which we have gone in aping the totalitarian system. The Supreme Court of California cast history aside and upheld, by a four to three vote, the exaction of the loyalty oath from the Unitarians, the Quakers, the Methodists, and all other church groups that seek a tax exemption. *First Unitarian Church* v. *Los Angeles*, 48 A.C. 417; *Peoples Church* v. *Los Angeles*, 48 A.C. 468; *First Methodist Church* v. *Harstmann*, 48 A.C. 470. As of the date of this writing (June, 1957) that is the only constitutional test of this kind of loyalty oath. In general, the courts have not been sympathetic to the requirement of an oath from tenants of public housing projects. The Supreme Court of Wisconsin has, indeed, held that the exaction of such an oath is an unconstitutional infringement of the tenants' rights under the First Amendment. *Lawson* v. *Housing Authority*, 270 Wis. 269.

I doubt if the non-communist oath results in the disclosure of communists.

"Both in demanding an oath and in taking it, we perpetuate the ridiculous illusion that enemies can be kept out through this prayer-wheel system. The fact is that deliberate traitors and subversives are the very ones who are not afraid to disguise their motivations and hide their intentions behind prescribed formulations. Nor are they afraid of perjury charges. They feel no hesitation in signing an oath if it is opportune for them to do so. For them, words and oaths are only tools which have no binding moral value." Meerloo, *The Rape of the Mind*, 251.

Those who refuse to take such an oath are often eminent

people who object to the requirement of the oath, although they could truthfully sign it. An organization that uses the non-communist oath does not lose subversives—it loses qualified men who do not believe that a teacher or employee should be singled out and made to forswear a course of past conduct. The casualties inflicted by the test oath are in the main not suffered by those at whom the salvo is aimed.

The exculpatory oath and the test oath are extremely unwise choices to determine qualifications for employment. Procedures may be set up to establish a lawyer's qualifications to practice law, a teacher's competence to teach, or a citizen's fitness for government employment. The test oath and the exculpatory oath do not materially aid the inquiry.

When these oaths relate to past conduct, or to matters of conscience and belief, our history and heritage are on the side of the man who, like freeborn John Lilburne, refuses the oath.

V. RELIGIOUS FREEDOM

Dean Pound, in *The Spirit of the Common-Law* (1921), traces the Puritan influence in our constitutional law and in our common law. The Puritan, he says, "put individual conscience and individual judgment in the first place." *Id.*, p. 42. All aspects of the First Amendment emphasize that choice. None underlines it more than the guarantee of religious freedom.

The provision of the First Amendment that "Congress shall make no law respecting an establishment of religion, or prohibiting the free exercise thereof" was a marked break with tradition. In colonial days bitter religious conflicts raged here. Most of the American colonies carried anti-Catholic legislation on their books. Some also discriminated against Jews and atheists. Some colonies were founded to protect only one religious sect. Thus Massachusetts in the early days allowed people to be tried for sedition when they criticized what the majority called the true faith. The penalty was banishment. Maryland made the denial that Jesus was the Son of God a capital offense. Some of the colonies required public officials to satisfy a religious test in order to hold office. Moreover, a majority of the colonies had an established church. That one church was supported by taxation; and only its clergy could officiate at marriages and baptisms. The established church frequently represented a minority of the people. Yet all were taxed to support it.

In spite of the discriminatory laws against some religions and the effort to produce uniformity in religious thought, the number of sects grew and flourished. As a result, toleration one for the other became a necessity. Moreover, a large percentage of the colonial people belonged to no church at all. Many of them became articulate opponents of levying taxes to support one church or all churches. Many opposed measures aimed at making the citizen revere any one religious doctrine. It was in this atmosphere of great diversity of religious views, of intense conflict and rivalry, that men like Madison and Jefferson worked for disestablishment, for separation of church and state, and for liberty of conscience. The reasons for their success were several and varied. But certain it is that out of the welter of doctrinal disputes and religious persecutions and discriminations there quietly and quickly emerged a declaration of faith in religious tolerance and in the separation of church and state. It was a revolution achieved without bitter or bloody conflicts. The result was a regime of religious tolerance seldom witnessed on the earth.

The religious freedom which the First Amendment protects has many facets:

1. No sectarian authority shares in the power of government nor sits in its councils.

2. Government has no directive influence in any of the affairs of any church.

3. Citizens are not taxed for the support of any religious institutions and no church has any claim on any of the public revenues.

4. People can belong to any church they desire—or to none at all; and no one is bound to have a ceremony such as marriage performed by any sectarian authority.

5. In disputes between sects or factions of a church over the management of church affairs the civil courts apply not the law applicable to secular affairs but the law that the governing bodies of the church have provided to govern their internal affairs.

138

6. Public schools are not proper agencies for religious education, though there is no constitutional reason why the state cannot adjust the schedules of the public schools to allow time for the students to get religious instruction elsewhere.

7. Parents and children have the privilege of patronizing private religious schools, rather than public ones, if they so desire.

8. An exercise or ritual may not be exacted by the state from an individual, if it runs counter to his religious convictions.

9. Religious liberty includes not only the conventional methods of worship but the unorthodox as well, such as distributing religious literature from door to door.

10. No license may be exacted by the state for the performance of any religious exercise nor a tax imposed on it.

11. Although the matter has not been authoritatively decided, it would seem that religious liberty extends to atheists as well as to theists, to those who find their religion in ethics and morality, rather than in a Supreme Being.

12. What may be pagan exercises to one person may be a devotional to another. In general it is no business of the government what rite or practice a person selects as a part of his religious belief; and he may not be punished for practicing or avowing it.

It is around this last category that some of the most

bitter controversies over the right to be let alone have raged. Ours is a society where the dictates of religion and conscience hold a high place. Performance of civic duty and obedience to law also have their place. It is when these values collide that the meaning of the guarantee of religious freedom is called in question.

Board of Education v. *Barnette,* 319 U.S. 624, upheld the right of school children to refuse to salute the flag where to do so was to violate their religious scruples. *Hamilton* v. *Regents,* 293 U.S. 245, held that a State could refuse to admit students to its universities unless they agreed to take military training, even though they had religious scruples against such training. *In re Summers,* 325 U.S. 538, held that Illinois could bar a man from practicing law who had religious scruples against serving in the armed services and who believed in passive resistance. And *Reynolds* v. *United States,* 98 U.S. 145, and *Davis* v. *Brown,* 133 U.S. 333, held that it was no defense to a prosecution for bigamy that polygamy was part of the religion of the defendants.

It is obvious that an individual should not have the final say on what is "religion" within the meaning of the First Amendment. Some review and expression of disinterested judgment are necessary. Otherwise minor things, such as obeying traffic signals, or important civic duties, such as the payment of taxes, could be blown up into forbidden exactions by calling them infringements on religious liberty. Likewise, practices that are abhorrent to civilized people, such as human sacrifices, are beyond the pale. None would go so far as to include them in religion. Polygamy, to which many millions of people in the Middle East and Asia are committed, may be more debatable. It is, however, alien to the moral code of the West. To our community it does no violence to place polygamy outside the scope of religious practices so far as First Amendment rights are concerned.

Yet if saluting the flag can amount to bearing false testimony to one's religion, it is difficult to see why military training may not also amount to the same thing. Religious conviction that military training is a sin is as much within the grasp of reason as religious conviction that saluting the flag is bowing to a graven image. Rational minds can comprehend both attitudes.

In re Summers, 325 U.S. 561, represents a break with the First Amendment. Summers was a conscientious objector, so classified under the Selective Training and Service Act. As I have said, he believed in passive resistance. He was deeply opposed to using force even to meet aggression, and would not serve in either the military or police forces. Illinois, therefore, refused to admit him to the Bar; and the Court sustained that action, holding it was not in violation of the First Amendment.

In re Summers teaches that, in spite of the First Amendment, a man fully qualified to practice law may be denied the privilege of practicing law when he takes the words of the New Testament literally and believes in passive resistance.

Rendering military service is not the only way to serve one's country in time of war. Manpower is then mobilized for all major activities. Whether one serves in agriculture, industry, medical care, or civil defense, he aids his nation in its critical hour. Certainly our experience has shown that honoring the claim of the conscientious objector has in no way crippled our war efforts. In principle both saluting the flag and rendering military service would seem to have equal claim to those privileges that are protected by the First Amendment.

To be sure, the *Hamilton* case did not require all citizens of a certain age to submit to military training. It prescribed military training as a course of study for those who chose to attend a state university. Military training thus could be avoided by not enrolling in the university. But that difference does not seem to be one of substance. Theoretically the students in the *Barnette* case could avoid the flag salute by attending private schools. In each it seems that the state was attaching a condition to the enjoyment of one of the privileges it extended to citizens—a condition that collided with the First Amendment. If one condition were to fall because it was unconstitutional, the other should likewise.

Yet the *Hamilton* case has grown in stature over the years and has come to stand for the proposition that religious scruples are no barrier either to military training or to military service.

Traditionally, the conscientious objector has been granted an exemption by the legislature—an exemption which in origin allowed the person drafted to supply a substitute or pay money necessary to hire one. That was the device used in the Civil War. Later statutes contained exemptions for the conscientious objector. The 1917 Act exempted ordained ministers, students preparing for the ministry, and members of well-recognized religious sects whose principles forbid its members to participate in war in any form and whose religious convictions are against war or participation in war. Under that law the exemption extended only to persons who belonged to a group which was against war and whose own religious scruples accorded with the group. The lone dissenter would not be included in the exemption. The 1940 Act, as amended in 1948, made individual religious conviction the test, whether or not the individual belonged to an organized religious group. But the religious conviction test was somewhat narrowly defined to mean "an individual's belief in a relation to a Supreme Being involving duties superior to those arising from any human relation, but does not include essentially political, sociological, or philosophical views or a merely personal moral code."

If the exemption of the conscientious objector is not a matter of grace, but protected by the First Amendment, then it seems clear that it is irrelevant that he is not a member of a religious group but stands on his own. It likewise seems irrelevant that he does not believe in a Supreme Being. Freedom of religion should include freedom to be an atheist, an agnostic, or a spiritualist.

The First Amendment is not concerned with dogma alone, but with the conscience. The classical statement is that of Martin Luther. He told the Diet of Worms on April 18, 1521, when asked if he would recant his writings:

"Since Your Majesty and Your Lordships ask for a

143

plain answer, I will give you one without either horns or teeth. Unless I am convicted by Scriptures or by right reason (for I trust neither in Popes nor in councils, since they have often erred and contradicted themselves)— unless I am thus convinced, I am bound by the texts of the Bible, my conscience is captive to the Word of God. I neither can nor will recant anything, since it is neither right nor safe to act against conscience. God help me, Amen."

When the conscience of man cries out against taking a certain step or performing a certain act, he should have the same protection under the First Amendment as those whose conscientious objections have been formalized into a creed.

VI. THE DIGNITY OF MAN

In discussing the right to be let alone, I have spoken so far mostly of opinions, beliefs, and matters of conscience. But the right to privacy covers another domain. I refer to the sanctity of the home and the right of the citizen to be unmolested there, either by peeping toms or by lawless police on a raid. I refer also to the sanctity of the person and the indignity suffered when a lawless hand is laid upon him. Even the humblest of citizens has the same dignity before the law as the most powerful. Each is entitled to the same protection, the same deference, the same immunity from lawless action. The police may not lay a heavy hand on the citizen. They may not beat him or torture him or hold him incommunicado. Man is a child of God entitled to dignified treatment. The state is the servant of the citizen, not the all-powerful being that can require the citizen to do its bidding or suffer the consequences. The police who torture prisoners can be brought to account.

That is the theory of our way of life; and we have been faithful to it to a degree. But in a measure our practices have not conformed to our ideal.

1. SELF-INCRIMINATION: The Fifth Amendment provides that "No person . . . shall be compelled in any criminal case to be a witness against himself." The privilege against self-incrimination helps protect anyone—guilty and innocent alike—from the prosecutor, the police, and even from Congress and the courts. It outlaws compulsion in any form utilized to make a man a witness against himself or to furnish the evidence used to convict him of crime.

The Fifth Amendment outlaws torture. Though torture was long used to solve crimes, experience proved that it was not an honorable way for government to deal with its citizens. Even the miserable creature who has committed a heinous crime is a human being. Torture does not comport with the dignity of man.

But the protection of the Fifth Amendment transcends the use of torture by the police. It outlaws all forms of physical, legal, or moral compulsion utilized to make a man convict himself. The aversion to that type of compulsion,

which culminated in the privilege against self-incrimination, has deep roots in our history. I have already mentioned part of that history, which can be found in the
struggle against the oath *ex officio*, the trial of John Lilburne, the repeated struggles—from the time of Queen
Elizabeth down to the present—against the imposition of
test oaths. Those who would attach a sinister meaning to
the invocation of the Fifth Amendment have forgotten
that history. For, from the beginning, the dignity of man
cried out against compulsion. If the individual's spirit of
liberty is to be kept alive, if government is to be civilized
in its relation to the citizen, no form of compulsion should
be used to exact evidence from him that might convict
him. This is the theory of the Fifth Amendment. It is why
Dean Griswold suggested that "the privilege against self-
incrimination is one of the great landmarks in man's struggle to make himself civilized."

Slochower v. *Board of Education*, 350 U.S. 551, is in that
tradition. It held that a State was not justified in discharg-
ing an employee merely because, in a federal investigation,
he invoked the privilege against self-incrimination when
asked about past membership in the Communist Party. Invocation of the privilege is not a confession of guilt. The
Fifth Amendment was designed for the protection of the
innocent as well as the guilty. As the Court in the *Slochower* case said, "A witness may have a reasonable fear of
prosecution and yet be innocent of any wrongdoing." *Id.*,
p. 557. The invocation of the privilege therefore is no measure of the fitness of a person for public employment.

The public is often unable to comprehend why a witness, either in court or before a congressional committee, invokes the privilege against self-incrimination in response to seemingly innocuous questions. The answer is apparent only to those versed in the law. The scope of the protection which the privilege affords is extremely broad. It extends to every question whose answer "would furnish a link in the chain of evidence needed to prosecute the claimant for a federal crime." *Hoffman* v. *United States*, 341 U.S. 479. A good example is the case of *Curcio* v. *United States*, 354 U.S. 118. Curcio was the secretary-treasurer of a local union who invoked the privilege in response to questions by a grand jury concerning the whereabouts of union books and records. Curcio could be required to produce the books, if he had them, since they were not his, but belonged to the union. For that reason, he could not invoke the privilege against self-incrimination as a ground for refusing to produce the union's records. But questions as to the whereabouts of those records stand on a different footing. As Mr. Justice Burton said for a unanimous Court, ". . . forcing the custodian to testify orally as to the whereabouts of nonproduced records requires him to disclose the contents of his own mind. He may be compelled to convict himself out of his own mouth. That is contrary to the spirit and letter of the Fifth Amendment." *Id.*, p. 128.

But the broad sweep of the privilege itself creates problems for the witness who must decide whether to answer a specific question. As noted, he is entitled to invoke the privilege in response to any question if his answer would furnish the prosecutor a link in a chain of proof to convict the witness of crime. But if he elects to answer one question which is part of that chain, he waives his right to invoke the privilege in response to further questions concerning more incriminating details. That was the situation in *Rogers* v. *United States*, 340 U.S. 367, where a divided Court decided that a witness who admitted association with the Communist Party could not refuse to answer further questions concerning her activities in connection with the Party. The danger is apparent: a witness may wholly waive the right to invoke the privilege by answering a question which would seem not incriminating on its face.

The situations are numerous where even a competent lawyer is not able to decide with certainty whether the answer to a particular question would constitute a waiver of the privilege, as in the *Rogers* case. Yet the decision to answer or not to answer must often be made on the spot. That is the reason why the witness' lawyer often advises his client to invoke the Fifth Amendment at the very threshold of the inquiry. This dilemma facing the witness is not always understood by those who denounce, ridicule, or attach a sinister meaning to the invocation of the Fifth Amendment's privilege against self-incrimination.

2. SEARCHES AND SEIZURES: The Constitution of Puerto Rico provides that "Wire-tapping is prohibited." Those few words give the right of privacy a protection it heretofore has never received. Our Fourth Amendment does not go that far. It only protects the people against "unreasonable searches and seizures" and provides that no search warrants shall issue except on probable cause and particularly

148

describing the place to be searched and the persons or things to be seized.

The history of this Amendment is a familiar one. In colonial days writs of assistance were issued, authorizing officers to search places of business and homes at any time. No showing was required that there were reasons to believe that the person whose place was searched had violated, or was violating, any law. The writs gave officials authority to ransack houses or places of business indiscriminately. It was against this practice that James Otis protested. It was out of that oppressive use of the search warrant that the Fourth Amendment was born.

The legal controversies over the application of that Amendment have been numerous. Every Fourth Amendment contest involves to a degree an issue of privacy. The right to be secure in one's own castle, the right to be free of snoopers, the right to keep the officers of the law out of one's bedroom and out of one's files are the values at stake in many of these contests. None has been more dramatic than the contests over wire-tapping.

The main struggle here has not been to prohibit wire-tapping absolutely, as Puerto Rico does, but to bring wire-tapping under the Fourth Amendment. That is to say, the controversy in the United States has been whether wire-tapping is a "search" within the meaning of the Amendment. If so, it requires a showing of probable cause to a magistrate that a crime has been or is being committed before a wire can be tapped. If not, it goes unregulated except as Congress or the States legislate concerning it.

To date the Court has been unwilling to bring wire-tap-

149

ping within the scope of the Fourth Amendment. It has held that the Fourth Amendment covers only a search of material things—"the person, the house, his papers or his effects." *Olmstead* v. *United States*, 277 U.S. 438, 464. Yet the degree of invasion of privacy which wire-tapping makes possible is greater than the ransacking of desks and of files which inflamed James Otis. With modern electronic devices, conversations within the home and the office can be recorded without tapping any wire. The intimacies of private life can be made public without a key being turned or a window being raised. And those who listen in may be private detectives and blackmailers, as well as law-enforcement officials.

Congress took steps to control the practice. It did not outlaw wire-tapping. But by the Communications Act of 1934, it made it unlawful for any person, not authorized by the sender, to intercept any communication and to divulge it. In cases construing the Act it was held that "any person" includes federal officers; and that evidence obtained from a defendant by wire-tapping cannot be used to convict him of a crime in the federal courts.

Despite the prohibitions imposed by the Communications Act, wire-tapping as a method of detecting crime is now used more and more. It is used both by officials and private parties to eavesdrop on conversations. Eavesdropping is the aspect of wire-tapping that made Justice Holmes call it "dirty business."

If wire-tapping were controlled by the Fourth Amendment, we would have made an important step forward toward controlling the practice. Then officers would make a search and seizure in the constitutional sense when they tapped wires and listened in on conversations. A warrant, issued on a showing of probable cause, would therefore be necessary if wires were to be tapped. As matters now stand, all controls over wire-tapping are a matter of legislative grace.

If wire-tapping were brought under the Fourth Amendment, an advance would be made in eliminating abuses. But the Fourth Amendment is not self-executing. The right of privacy which it protects is only secure when its prohibitions are respected by law-enforcement officers and enforced by the courts.

Many States have laws that prohibit wire-tapping. But they do not seem to be effective. The truth is that wire-tapping today is a plague on the nation. It is a far more serious intrusion on privacy than the general writs of assistance used in colonial days. Now all the intimacies of one's private life can be recorded. This is far worse than ransacking one's desk and closets. This is a practice that strikes as deep as an invasion of the confessional.

The judicial mood has not been libertarian. In *On Lee v. United States*, 343 U.S. 747, an agent, wired for sound, entered the place of business of a suspect and engaged him in conversation. The entire conversation was audited through a radio receiving set in the possession of another agent who remained outside. The conversation was admitted in evidence over the objection that this invasion of privacy violated the Fourth Amendment. The Court, speaking through Mr. Justice Jackson, overruled the ob-

jection, and extended the wire-tapping rule one step
further.

3. DUE PROCESS OF LAW: I have been speaking so far of
civil liberties in trials or proceedings before federal courts
or federal agencies. When we turn to state courts or state
agencies, we have a somewhat different problem. The
Fourteenth Amendment, which is applicable to the States,
forbids the taking of life, liberty, or property without "due
process of law." It has long been argued that "due process
of law," as used in the Fourteenth Amendment, includes
the guarantee of civil liberties contained in the Bill of
Rights, *i.e.*, the first eight Amendments. That argument has
been consistently rejected by the Court, though usually by
a divided vote. Some guarantees, *e.g.*, those contained in
the First Amendment, have been held to be protected by
"due process of law" as used in the Fourteenth Amendment. But other guarantees of the Bill of Rights, including
the one concerning self-incrimination, have been held to
be not so protected.

What then does "due process" as used in the Fourteenth
Amendment include? It includes those guarantees that are
"implicit in the concept of ordered liberty." *Palko* v. *Connecticut*, 302 U.S. 319, 325. It outlaws practices "repugnant
to the conscience of mankind." *Id.*, p. 323. That is a highly
subjective test, turning on the reactions of a majority of
the Court to particular practices.

The capricious results that sometimes obtain when
judges write their own reactions into "due process" are illustrated by *Irvine* v. *California*, 347 U.S. 128. This was a

state prosecution in which evidence against the defendant was obtained in flagrant violation of his rights of privacy. First the police made a key to his house. Then they bored a hole in the roof of the house. Using the key, they entered the house, installed a microphone, and ran wires through the hole in the roof to a nearby garage, where the police listened in relays. For a while the microphone was placed in the bedroom where the suspect and his wife slept. Later it was moved into the bedroom closet. When the police had all the evidence they needed, they used the key to enter the home to arrest the suspect. Though they had no search warrant, they ransacked the house. A divided Court, speaking through Mr. Justice Jackson, upheld the conviction. This method of obtaining evidence was held not to violate "due process," though a more dramatic invasion of privacy is difficult to imagine.

When we turn to the other police practices violative of the dignity of man, "due process" remains an uncertain, evanescent concept. When police officers use force to put a stomach pump into a prisoner and use the evidence obtained to convict him, "due process" is violated. To the Court this is "conduct that shocks the conscience." *Rochin* v. *California*, 342 U.S. 165, 172. Yet blood taken from an unconscious man and used in a state trial to convict him of drunken driving was held to be properly admissible. That method of tampering with the body of an unconscious person accused of crime was held not violative of "due process." *Breithaupt* v. *Abram*, 352 U.S. 432.

On the other hand, all are agreed that confessions exacted from prisoners by force violate "due process" and therefore cannot be used in state prosecutions. These inquisitional practices that wring confessions from an accused have been outlawed by the Supreme Court as evidence in state prosecutions, whether force was used to exact them or whether subtler methods were employed. We reject the rack, the thumbscrew, and the wheel, because they affront the dignity of man. Torture may be a short cut for getting at the truth. But it is not a civilized practice.

As Beccaria, the eighteenth century Italian legal philosopher, wrote, torture is an "infamous test of truth."

A devilish way Hitler used to exact confessions was to drill on a live tooth while the victim was strapped in a dentist's chair. That is one of the most horrible practices the ingenuity of man has devised. But Hitler had no monopoly on it. In the 1930's some American police stations used the same technique.

The Wickersham Commission reported in 1931 that the third degree was widespread in this country. Prolonged detention, holding people *incommunicado*, the use of threats, protracted questioning, and various forms of physical brutality, ranging from beating to torture, were the methods used.

Disclosure and denunciation of the third degree do not mean, however, that the practice ends. There is convincing evidence that the third degree still flourishes in the police stations of the nation. The methods may not be as crude as before. But the recurring appearance of the problem in the flow of cases suggests that the practice has gone underground, so to speak, taking on new forms.

154

4. DETENTION OF SUSPECTS: The prolonged detention of suspects has been a time-honored practice of the police; and it has been used as a method of exacting confessions from them. One who is held *incommunicado* without benefit of family, friends, or counsel to aid him and to advise him is easy prey for the police. He can be questioned for hours or days on end by relays of officers. He may even be beaten or tortured.

When the police hold a man *incommunicado* the opportunities for coercion are great. Proof of it is always difficult. There is the word of the accused against the word of the police. The judge—or the jury—that has to decide where the truth lies often has a difficult, if not impossible, task.

One solution is to exclude from the trial any statement made by the accused to the police during his detention. That is the course India, following the British precedent, has adopted in her Code of Criminal Procedure. The rule governing the federal courts in the United States is different. Congress has long provided that people arrested are to be taken before a magistrate for a hearing, for commitment, or for bail. That mandate is now embodied in the Federal Rules of Criminal Procedure which direct federal officers to take a suspect who is arrested before a magistrate "without unnecessary delay." The policy behind that rule is to prevent the secret interrogation of people accused of crime.

In *McNabb* v. *United States*, 318 U.S. 332, the Court held that disregard by federal officers of that rule concerning detention of a suspect renders inadmissible any statement taken from him during the period of his unlawful detention. The rule of the *McNabb* case is designed to insure that the police will not illegally hold a suspect *incommunicado* in the hopes of extracting a confession from him. The officers who do illegally detain an accused are denied the fruits of their acts.

The requirement of the Federal Rules of Criminal Procedure, that the accused be committed "without unreasonable delay," permits the police to hold a man long enough to perform necessary police functions, such as photographing and fingerprinting him. The purpose of an arrest should not be to interrogate the suspect or to secure evidence against him. Its aim should be to bring him before a judicial officer (who determines whether he should be held) and to insure that he will respond to the criminal charge. As Mr. Justice Frankfurter, writing for the Court in *Mallory* v. *United States*, 354 U.S. 449, said, any delay in arraignment "must not be of a nature to give opportunity for the extraction of a confession."

The rule of the *McNabb* case does not impose a constitutional requirement. The States are free to admit or exclude confessions obtained while the accused was illegally detained by the police, absent proof of coercion.

While the *McNabb* rule is the ideal, it is, I fear, not greatly respected in practice. Detention of suspects for secret interrogations continues both at the federal and at the state level.

Real reforms must come from within the police system. That requires an educational program that pounds into the consciousness of our people the sanctity of the dignity of man. It also requires a press that is alert to the infringement of the rights of privacy.

The problem is one of education, whether we speak of coerced confessions, wire-tapping, or other invasions of privacy. Courts can make their pronouncements and control individual cases. But the use of totalitarian methods will persist unless there is a lively educational program that teaches the dignity of man.

We are told about crime and the need for law enforcement. We often think more in terms of detection and punishment than in the means employed. There is no organized group, no articulate minority that keeps alive the need for protecting the accused. People whose homes are searched are the lowly, not the high. It is the unknown person who is tortured by the police. The prominent and the powerful people among us do not suffer the main invasions of privacy that take place. As Justice Black said in *Chambers* v. *Florida*, 309 U.S. 227, 238, ". . . they who have suffered most from secret and dictatorial proceedings have almost always been the poor, the ignorant, the numerically weak, the friendless, and the powerless." If they are to be protected, the public opinion of the community, as well as the courts, must be enlightened.

The means are all important in a civilized society. It may seem unimportant that a miserable person is forced to confess to a crime. But in the sweep of history, a nation that accepts that practice as normal, a country that engages in wire-tapping, a people that exalts the ends over the means have no claim to a position of moral leadership among the nations.

VII. THE RIGHT TO DEFY
AN UNCONSTITUTIONAL STATUTE

There are circumstances where the otherwise absolute obligation of the law is tempered by exceptions for individual conscience. As in the case of the conscientious objector to military service, the exception may be recognized by statute or, as in the case of the flag salute for school children, it may be required by the First Amendment. But in countless other situations the fact that conscience counsels violation of the law can be no defense. Those are the situations in which the citizen is placed in the dilemma of being forced to choose between violating the dictates of his conscience or violating the command of positive law.

The problem is age-old. In Sophocles' play, Antigone had this choice to make. She chose to follow the dictates of her conscience, attempting to bury the body of her brother, Polynices, rather than conform to the edict of the tyrant, Creon, that the corpse remain unburied. Socrates, convicted of corrupting the youth of Athens, refused to "hold his tongue," preferring to face death. Even Hobbes, who wrote that civil obedience is the highest duty of a citizen, recognized that a point could be reached where conscience would demand that the command of the leviathan state must be disobeyed. But for Hobbes, civil disobedience was not justified unless to obey would be to lose the right to eternal salvation after death.

The moral right to defy an unjust law was certainly not unknown in the American colonies. The Puritans fled England after they had defied the English sovereigns by adhering to their forms of worship. John Locke, an intellectual father of the American Revolution, wrote that, if the sovereign should require anything which appears unlawful to the private person, he is not obliged to obey that law against his conscience. Locke's philosophy found expression in the Declaration of Independence.

Emerson wrote that "no greater American existed than Thoreau." Thoreau's insistence on his right to lead his own life and to resist the encroachment of government was typically American. In 1846, he refused to pay the town tax because he disapproved of the purposes for which the money was to be spent. For this, he spent a night in jail. He was released only after a friend had "interfered" and paid the tax. His short imprisonment resulted in Thoreau's dramatic essay on civil disobedience, where he insisted that he had the right to disobey an unjust law. "Under a government which imprisons any unjustly," he wrote, "the true place for a just man is also a prison."

Thoreau's writings had a great impact on Gandhi. Gandhi's concept of *satyagraba* was one which championed the moral right to disregard an unjust law and undergo the penalty for its breach. He wrote:

"The law-breaker breaks the law surreptitiously and tries to avoid the penalty; not so the civil resister. He

159

ever obeys the laws of the state to which he belongs, not out of fear of the sanctions, but because he considers them to be good for the welfare of society. But there come occasions, generally rare, when he considers certain laws to be so unjust as to render obedience to them a dishonour. He then openly and civilly breaks them and quietly suffers the penalty of their breach. And in order to register his protest against the action of the law-givers, it is open to him to withdraw his co-operation from the state by disobeying such other laws whose breach does not involve moral turpitude."

Unless the law applies with equal force to those who dissent from it, there can be no ordered society. The choice given the individual is not to obey the law or to violate it with impunity, but to obey the law or incur the punishment for disobedience. Socrates recognized the obligation of the law which had unjustly sentenced him to die, when he explained to Crito that he would not flee from his punishment. He recognized that his choice was to incur the punishment of the law rather than conform to it, but did not contend that he was above the law. Locke, too, observed that the "private judgment of any person concerning a law enacted in public matters, for the public good, does not take away the obligation of that law, nor deserve a dispensation." Rousseau, who had defended the right to resist unjust law, still observed that no individual in a democracy should have the right to be above the law. Both Thoreau and Gandhi recognized that disobedience of the law may be punished.

These two values, the right of the individual to follow his own conscience and the right of society to promulgate rules for the orderly conduct of its affairs, are sometimes antagonistic. American democracy is not the leviathan state which Hobbes pictured. Our society is built upon the premise that it exists only to aid the fullest individual achievement of which each of its members is capable. Our starting point has always been the individual, not the state. Nevertheless, democracy is built upon the rule of the majority, and a civilized society requires orderly rules, applicable to all alike. If a statute is otherwise valid, the law does not consider the moral values which led to its disobedience.

But the Puritan tradition of the citizen's right to shake his fist at the legislature has found its place in American law in the right to defy an unconstitutional statute. An unconstitutional statute is a lawless act by the legislature. The humblest citizen, confronted by all the forces of the state which insist that he must obey the law, may take matters into his own hands, defy an unconstitutional statute, and risk the outcome on the ultimate decision of the courts. He may forsake the orderly processes of society and proceed as if the statute does not exist. That was Jefferson's attitude toward the Alien and Sedition Laws. On July 22, 1804, he wrote:

". . . I discharged every person under punishment or prosecution under the sedition law, because I considered, and now consider, that law to be a nullity, as absolute and as palpable as if Congress had ordered us to

161

fall down and worship a golden image; and that it was as much my duty to arrest its execution at every stage, as it would have been to have rescued from the fiery furnace those who should have been cast into it for refusing to worship the image. It was accordingly done in every instance, without asking what the offenders had done, or against whom they had offended, but whether the pains they were suffering were inflicted under the pretended sedition law."

The clearest example of an individual's right to ignore an unconstitutional ordinance is in the area of prior restraint upon First Amendment freedoms, which I have discussed in the first lecture. *Thomas* v. *Collins,* 323 U.S. 516, involved a statute which required a labor organizer to obtain a license before he could address an assembly of laborers. He ignored that statute and spoke. His conviction for speaking without a license was overturned because the statute constituted an infringement of his right to speak. He was not required to submit to the invalid ordinance, apply for the license, and be refused the right to speak, before he was allowed to challenge the validity of the statute. Under the principle of *Thomas* v. *Collins,* a minister who is required to get a license to address his flock could not be convicted for preaching without a license.

Of course, if an individual violates a statute under the mistaken view that it is unconstitutional, he may be punished. As Chief Justice Stone once said, "There is no freedom to conspire to violate a statute with impunity merely because its constitutionality is doubted. The prohibition of the statute is infringed by the intended act in any case, and the law imposes its sanctions unless the doubt proves to be well founded." *Keegan* v. *United States*, 325 U.S. 478, 505. The citizen who defies the statute takes the risk that he is mistaken. But if his views of the Constitution are accepted, he goes free.

A striking analogy may be found in the Articles of the Uniform Code of Military Justice. In the Armed Forces, discipline and obedience to orders are of primary importance. Under military discipline, respect for authority is the prime virtue. But, under Articles 90 through 92 of the Uniform Code, an American serviceman has the absolute right to disobey any unlawful order of a superior officer, for he is punished only for disobedience of a *lawful* order. A recent decision of the United States Court of Military Appeals demonstrates that this right has real value. An airman stationed in Japan, suspected of using narcotics, had been ordered by his squadron commander to furnish a urine specimen for chemical analysis. Although the airman was warned of the possibility of court-martial for failure to comply, he refused to do so. He was court-martialed for willful disobedience of the command of a superior officer. The United States Court of Military Appeals set aside the conviction, holding that the order was unlawful because it compelled the airman to furnish evidence against himself. *United States* v. *Jordan*, 7 U.S.C.M.A. 452. This was an order from a superior officer, with all the force of military discipline behind it; yet, under the Uniform Code of Military Justice, it could be disobeyed with impunity because the order itself was not legal.

There will be specific instances where most people will agree that the individual's right to defy even an unconstitutional statute may be denied because of the interest of society in the continued conduct of the processes of government. For example, a taxpayer can be required to pay an unconstitutional tax and sue for its return. If he prevails, he has only been temporarily deprived of the use of his money. For this he can be compensated. On the other hand, if every taxpayer refused to pay his taxes, the business of government would grind to a halt.

There has developed, however, in recent years a tendency to require the citizen to obey an extreme ordinance or statute, even though it is unconstitutional. The rights of the individual are then sacrificed to the interests of orderly conduct of the processes of government. The Court has gone far in requiring that sacrifice. The most striking example is *Poulos* v. *New Hampshire*, 345 U.S. 395. Jehovah's Witnesses had been arbitrarily denied a license to speak in a public park. The Court, in affirming their convictions for holding a religious meeting without the required license, held that their remedy for violation of their right to speak was to proceed as required by state law to compel issuance of the license.

The *Poulos* decision is a significant departure from prior decisions which have allowed the individual the right to resist the unconstitutional demands of government. The right to speak, guaranteed by the First Amendment, was sacrificed to the delays, the expense, and the necessities of pursuing the processes of an "orderly society." *Id.*, p. 409.

The risk—the great and agonizing danger—in situations of this kind is that the citizen will be caught in the treadmill of an elusive administrative remedy. While he pursues it, his constitutional rights are denied. And it may take so much time to go through the intricate administrative system with all of its hearings and appeals that any relief will come too late and the great occasion, when the right to speak, to worship, or to assemble might have been enjoyed, will be lost.

The right to defy an unconstitutional statute has its roots in our traditions of individualism and in our mistrust of the uncontrolled power of the state. That mistrust was written into numerous limitations on governmental power contained in the Constitution. The right to ignore a statute that is unconstitutional is a reflection of those limitations. Like them, it says—so far government may go and no farther.

I have said enough to indicate that the right to be let alone, though greatly impaired in recent years, still clamors for recognition. It is a sturdy part of our heritage, more American than European, more Western than Eastern. It cannot be easily stamped out on this continent, for it is a part of all of us. It can be eroded and depreciated. But it will always be one of our great rallying points.

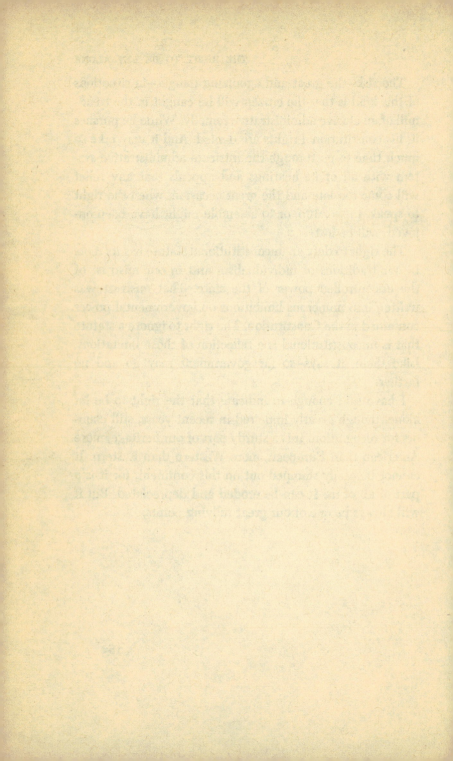

The Civilian Authority

I. THE AVERSION TO THE MILITARY

There are many myths about the Magna Carta which the barons wrung from King John in 1215. Certainly it became over the centuries something vastly different than it was in the beginning. Yet it stated in 1215 some principles that grew and flourished and in time became the fundamentals on which our Western democracies rest. One of these was the proposition that the political authority of the nation is subordinate to the law.

Magna Carta declared:

"No freeman shall be taken, or imprisoned, or disseized, or outlawed, or exiled, or in any way harmed—nor will we go upon or send upon him—save by the lawful judgment of his peers or by the law of the land.

"To none will we sell, to none deny or delay, right or justice."

As Winston Churchill has said, "The leaders of the barons in 1215 groped in the dim light towards a fundamental principle. Government must henceforward mean something more than the arbitrary rule of any man, and custom and the law must stand even above the King. It was this idea, perhaps only half understood, that gave unity and force to the barons' opposition and made the Charter which they now demanded imperishable." 1 *A History of the English-Speaking Peoples* (1956), p. 253.

On this continent, the struggle against the British was essentially a struggle for a government of laws. The idea was eloquently stated in the *Quebec Letter*, two years before the Declaration of Independence:

> ". . . the first grand right, is that of the people having a share in their own government by their representatives chosen by themselves, and, in consequence, of being ruled by *laws*, which they themselves approve, not by *edicts of men* over whom they have no controul."

One phase of that historic struggle—to create a government of laws, not of men—was the effort to bring the military under civilian control. There were many stages in that development.

In 1628 the Petition of Right complained of commissions issued by the Crown which authorized the trial and punishment of civilians as well as soldiers "according to the Justice of martial law." It was not the suppression of revolts by military force that was objected to; it was the punishment of offenders by military tribunals. The famous Bill of Rights of 1689 was another significant milestone, for it contained the declaration "That the raising or keeping a standing army within the Kingdome in time of peace, unless it be with consent of Parliament, is against law." There thus began, starting in 1689, a series of Mutiny Acts by which the army, as a national institution, became subject to annual approval by the Parliament.

The common law of England did not recognize courts-martial in times of peace. Military personnel, if they committed offenses, were triable by civil tribunals. As Macaulay wrote in *England in 1685* (1897), pp. 17–18:

> "The common law of England knew nothing of courts-martial, and made no distinction, in time of peace, between a soldier and any other subject; nor could the government then venture to ask even the most loyal parliament for a mutiny bill. A soldier, therefore, by knocking down his colonel, incurred only the ordinary penalties of assault and battery, and by refusing to obey orders, by sleeping on guard, or by deserting his colors, incurred no legal penalty at all."

There were many incidents in British history that resolved public opinion against a standing army. But none was more effective than Cromwell's dictatorship. In 1655 he divided England and Wales into eleven districts and placed each under control of a Major General. Churchill describes this military dictatorship as "naked if not wholly unashamed." 2 *A History of the English-Speaking Peoples*, p. 309. "The Major-Generals were given three functions—police and public order, the collection of special taxes upon acknowledged Royalists, and the strict enforcement of Puritan morality." *Id.*, pp. 309–310. Under Cromwell the army grew to forty thousand men "unequalled in fighting quality in the world." *Id.*, p. 330. Their oppressions and depredations were so great that when the Restoration came, "no standing army" became "the common watchword of all parties." *Id.*, p. 331.

Once a standing army was approved by Parliament, courts-martial followed. They were authorized by Parliament in the Mutiny Act of 1689 as indispensable for discipline. So it came to pass that the army could try its military personnel for offenses defined by the Parliament—the first being mutiny, sedition, and desertion.

Thus long before the American Revolution it was established in England that the army was subordinate to the civilian authority and that the laws for the government of the armed forces were written by the civilian authority.

When the American Revolution broke, the Continental Congress followed the British tradition. John Adams and Thomas Jefferson, a committee appointed to suggest Articles of War, recommended the British articles; and some forty of the hundred-odd that governed the British forces were adopted almost verbatim.

When the time came to draft the Constitution, the Framers not only had the benefit of British experience; they also had fresh personal experiences of their own. The Declaration of Independence complained of various acts of the King of England:

"He has kept among us, in times of peace, Standing Armies without the consent of our legislatures. He has affected to render the military independent of and superior to the Civil power. He has combined with others to subject us to a jurisdiction foreign to our constitution, and unacknowledged by our laws; giving his Assent to their acts of pretended legislation:—For quartering large bodies of armed troops among us:—For protecting them, by a mock trial, from punishment for any murders which they should commit on the inhabitants of these States. . . ."

The heart of the objection to rule by the military had been eloquently stated by Samuel Adams, in 1768, who protested against the British army stationed in Boston:

". . . let us then assert & maintain the honor—the dignity of free citizens and place the military, where all other men are, and where they always ought & always *will* be plac'd in every free country, *at the foot of the common law of the land*.—To submit to the civil magistrate in the *legal* exercise of power is forever the part of a good subject: and to *answer* the watchmen of the town in the night, may be the part of a good citizen, as well as to afford them all necessary countenance and support: But, to be called to account by a common soldier, or any soldier, is a badge of slavery which none but a *slave* will wear."

The country had been reminded of the threat of a standing army after the British had been defeated. Early in 1783 plans were on foot to have the Army take over the government. Millis, *Arms and Men* (1956), pp. 41-42. These plans were promoted by creditor groups who wanted a strong central government that could keep democratic tendencies under control. The promoters made a strong appeal to the prejudices of the army officers who had just complaints against the government concerning back pay and pensions. Washington nipped this plot in the bud. He addressed the officers at Newburgh on March 15, 1783, telling them that the idea of turning their arms against the government was "so shocking" "that humanity revolts at the idea." He asked them to express their "utmost horror and detestation of the man who wishes, under any specious pretences, to overturn the liberties of our country, and who wickedly attempts to open the flood gates of civil discord, and deluge our rising Empire in blood." Washington not only pleaded with the officers; he laid the whole matter before the Continental Congress. The officers rejected the proposal and it withered and died. Never since has the Army even ventured near to using its arms in domestic politics. The precedent set by Washington was the beginning of a great tradition that has become engrained in our institutions.

But the fear of a standing army lingered on. The Pennsylvania Constitution of 1776 stated that "as standing armies in the time of peace are dangerous to liberty, they ought not to be kept up." The Virginia Bill of Rights of 1776 made the same declaration. The idea was repeated over and again in these words—"A standing army, however necessary it may be, is always dangerous to the liberties of the people." This idea has been a militant one throughout almost every period of our history. Ekirch, *The Civilian and the Military* (1956). It survives today in the opposition that mounts to any suggestion for universal military service.

It also mounts in any attack on the militia. In our history

the militia has offset the regular army. The regular army was a national agency; the militia was always under the control of the several States. The militia evolved as the National Guard and today has as stout defenders as the militia had in 1776. When the National Guard was criticized by the Pentagon in 1957, many rushed to its defense, including Governor James E. Folsom of Alabama. The Governor said that if we had not had "the military of this nation in 49 different hands . . . that is 48 Governors and the President . . . we would have had a military dictatorship over 100 years ago. . . . Only the foresight of our fathers in placing in the elected officials of the people the authority of administering the National Guard has, in my opinion . . . prevented a military dictatorship in this country." He added, that support of the National Guard "will be a strong blow for the perpetration of democracy in our land and against that Federal clique of brass and bureaucrats seeking complete control of all military forces of our country, and against one-thumb rule."

The views of Governor Folsom reflect the fear of centralized military control that has appeared and reappeared throughout our history.

The fear of military supremacy even at the state level is also seen in the early constitutions of some of the States. Thus the 1776 Constitution of North Carolina provided that "the military should be kept under strict subordination to, and governed by, the civil power." The fear of a standing army and of military supremacy were powerful influences shaping the Constitution of the United States.

The fear of a centralized military force showed itself in

175

the debates on the Constitution in the ratifying conventions. In New Hampshire, New York, Rhode Island, Virginia, Pennsylvania, Maryland, and North Carolina there were proposals for amendments to the Constitution that would prohibit a standing army in time of peace, unless a high percentage of each House (usually two-thirds) concurred. One of the leading proponents of such an amendment was Patrick Henry, who sounded the alarm that a standing army might lead to despotism. But the views of Hamilton, Madison, and Marshall—that the federal government needs, in time of peace, powers that war would necessitate—prevailed.

The result of those expressed fears of the military was a division among several civilian agencies of the control over it.

The President—elected by the people—is the Commander-in-Chief of the Army and Navy and of the militia when called into actual service of the United States. The right of the people "to keep and bear arms" is recognized by the Second Amendment. The quartering of soldiers is regulated by the Third Amendment.

The militia is recognized as an arm of the States, though provisions are made for calling it into the service of the national government.

The national government, acting through Congress, can "provide for the common defence," declare war, raise and support armies, provide and maintain a navy, define and punish offenses against the law of nations, make rules for the government and regulation of the land and naval forces, and call forth the militia to be employed in the service of the United States. Congress has in addition the fulsome power to make all laws "necessary and proper" for carrying into execution the delegated powers. As a curb on the Army (but not the Navy) a device was borrowed from the English Mutiny Acts: no Army appropriation "shall be for a longer term than two years."

There are other ways in which the civilian authority is made superior to the military. By law, the Secretaries in charge of the various branches of the Armed Services must be civilians—a requirement that Congress by a special Act waived to allow General George C. Marshall to serve in the Cabinet. And in the Uniform Code of Military Justice, enacted in 1950, a court composed of civilians and designated as a Court of Military Appeals was made the agency of final review of questions of law arising in cases from courts-martial. Moreover, Congress has provided in the Selective Service Acts that the hand of the Army court-martial does not reach the draftee until and unless he is "actually inducted" into the Army, that for failure or refusal to be inducted he is triable not by the military but by the civil courts. *Billings* v. *Truesdell*, 321 U.S. 542. Before the soldier is actually in the Armed Services the civilian authority retains jurisdiction over him to the exclusion of the military; and after he is in, the civilian court has the final review over the action of the military authorities in disciplining or punishing him.

Two episodes illustrate the deep-seated reluctance of this nation to surrender power to the military establishment.

First, our courts-martial had no jurisdiction to try soldiers for murders committed by them until Congress in 1863 enacted a statute conferring such jurisdiction. Prior to that time, if a soldier committed murder, only state courts had jurisdiction over the offense. The American tradition has long been hostile "to any interference by the military with the regular administration of justice in the civil courts." *Coleman* v. *Tennessee*, 97 U.S. 509, 514.

Second, civilian witnesses before courts-martial could not be forced to testify prior to 1901. In that year Congress passed a law making it their duty to testify. But Congress did not give the power to punish them to the military. Rather, it made them punishable in the civil courts. And that is the law today.

II. REVIEW BY CIVILIAN COURTS

A word should be said covering the relationship between the civil courts and military courts. The Supreme Court has jurisdiction granted it by Congress to review decisions of state courts and decisions of the lower federal courts. But Congress has never given the Court power to sit in review of decisions of military courts. The appellate jurisdiction of the Court is determined not by the Constitution but by Congress. *Ex parte McCardle*, 7 Wall. 506. Since Congress has not given the Court power to review directly military courts, it is barred from entertaining an appeal even where it appears that the military have run rampant and acted unconstitutionally. See *Ex parte Vallandigham*, 1 Wall. 243. The courts do have some control over the military tribunals. But that control is exceedingly limited.

The primary control which civilian courts have over military tribunals is that granted by the ancient writ of habeas corpus. It tests only the jurisdiction of the military tribunal to act, not the correctness of its rulings nor the propriety of its action. Flagrant violation of the law governing courts-martial will at times go to the question of jurisdiction. For example, a denial of an opportunity to the accused to tender the defense of insanity would be a denial of due process which could be challenged by habeas corpus, as indicated in *Whelchel* v. *McDonald*, 340 U.S. 122, 124. Habeas corpus is also available where punishment is imposed for an act not made illegal by Congress. But the civilian courts are not empowered to correct, through habeas corpus, mere irregularities or errors in the proceedings before the military tribunal.

The Constitution, in Article I, Section 9, provides that the writ shall not be suspended "unless when in cases of rebellion or invasion the public safety may require it." In the Civil War, Lincoln suspended the writ and Congress ratified his action. During that period, the civil courts were without any remedy to rectify wrongs done by the military. But apart from that extreme situation, the writ of habeas corpus is available to challenge the action of military tribunals.

A second remedy is a suit for damages against the officers who carry out the decision of a military tribunal. That was early settled by *Wise* v. *Withers,* 3 Cranch 331, 337, where Chief Justice Marshall said that a decision by a military tribunal, "in a case clearly without its jurisdiction, cannot protect the officer who executes it. The court and the officer are all trespassers." That was an action for damages brought by a justice of the peace against an officer who seized the justice's goods to pay a fine levied by the military. Since the justice was exempt by law from military service, those who sought to subject him to it acted unlawfully and were liable to him for damages.

There is a third remedy available in a narrow group of cases. Where the military act unlawfully in cashiering an officer, he may maintain suit in the Court of Claims against the United States to recover his back pay. Such a suit was maintained in *Runkle* v. *United States,* 122 U.S. 543, where an officer was cashiered by a court-martial without confirmation by the President, as required by the Articles of War. A suit for back pay was also successfully maintained in *United States* v. *Brown,* 206 U.S. 240, where an unauthorized person—without whom there would have been no court as required by the Articles of War—sat on the court-martial that cashiered the officer. The action of a court-martial constituted in violation of the Articles of War is void. But in suits for damages or for back pay mere irregularities in the procedure of the court-martial are not sufficient to warrant recovery in the civil court. For the civil court to give a remedy, it must appear that the military court was not legally organized or that it had no jurisdiction over the offense or over the person of the accused, or that in some fundamental manner it departed from the procedure prescribed for it by the Congress. In other words, whether the remedy sought is by habeas corpus, by a suit for damages, or by a suit for back pay, the scope of review in the civil court is of a narrow compass. In each it reaches only questions that go to jurisdiction—not the merits nor procedural irregularities.

Yet this rather narrow control which the civil courts have over the military courts is a vital one. It insures that the military will act within the area assigned to it by Congress and the Constitution. It insures that the military's own judicial system will remain subject to ultimate civilian control on basic issues.

III. JURISDICTION OF MILITARY TRIBUNALS OVER CIVILIANS

By Article I, Section 8, of the Constitution, Congress has the power to make "rules for the government and regulation of the land and naval forces." The Fifth Amendment excepts "cases arising in the land or naval forces, or in the militia when in actual service in time of war or public danger" from the requirement that there be an indictment by a grand jury before there can be a federal prosecution. So far as cases "arising in the land or naval forces" are concerned, the power of Congress extends to the establishment of a system of military justice that is applicable in time of peace as well as in war. For the phrase "when in actual service in time of war or public danger" is applicable only to the militia. It is with both groups of cases—those "arising in the land or naval forces" and those in the militia "when in actual service in time of war or public danger"—that the Code of Military Justice, adopted by Congress, deals.

The Code of Military Justice contains many safeguards against arbitrary and oppressive action, apart from the machinery for review. In the more serious cases the accused is entitled to be represented by counsel even at the stage of the investigation. He is protected against double jeopardy. He may not be compelled to incriminate himself. He may demand that an enlisted man serve on the court and then one must serve unless conditions make it impossible. He is presumed innocent until his guilt is established beyond a reasonable doubt. In these and in other ways the code sets safeguards for trials by courts-martial and seeks to provide a procedure that will guarantee fair trials. Yet even so these trials fall short of constitutional standards. The standards provided in the code can be changed by another Congress to the extent that they rest not on the Constitution but on the generosity of the legislature.

It is clear that some guarantees of the Bill of Rights—notably indictment by grand jury provided by the Fifth Amendment and jury trial guaranteed by the Sixth—are not applicable to military trials, for the former is expressly excepted and the latter impliedly so. But the extent to which other procedural safeguards of the Bill of Rights—such as the right to confront witnesses, the right to a speedy trial, protection against double jeopardy, self-incrimination and coerced confessions—are *constitutionally* required in military trials has not been authoritatively determined. It would seem that a member of the Armed Forces would be entitled, under the Fifth Amendment, to the protection against being tried twice for the same offense. Situations in the field in time of war, however, may be such that a soldier can be constitutionally subjected to a second court-martial when tactical reasons make it impracticable to complete a prior trial, as *Wade* v. *Hunter*, 336 U.S. 684, shows. It would also seem that a confession exacted by torture and used against a soldier in a military trial would violate due process of law and vitiate the trial. But these and related questions have not yet been removed from the vague penumbra of the law.

Military trials are trials where swift and severe action is often necessary for discipline. The sentences in the past have been notorious for their harshness. They are often rendered by men who have no foundation in law or in the democratic tradition of law administration. On the other hand, civil courts established under Article III of the Constitution are manned by judges who have been scrutinized for their abilities for the post and who have been appointed for life. As noted, the military trial lacks the safeguard of the jury trial which is guaranteed by the Constitution. The jury trial is the institution through which the community sense of justice has through the years tempered the strictness of the law. Juries have sometimes inflicted injustices. But in our long history they have usually brought to judgment the quality of mercy that courts-martial do not often show.

The difference between civil courts and courts-martial was emphasized by General Sherman, who said: "The object of the civil law is to secure to every human being in a community all the liberty, security and happiness possible, consistent with the safety of all. The object of military law is to govern armies composed of strong men, so as to be capable of exercising the largest measure of force at the will of the nation. These objects are as wide apart as the poles, and each requires its own separate system of laws —statute and common." 1 *Journal Military Serv. Inst.* (1880), p. 130.

The moral is that sedulous care should be taken to restrict and confine the "cases arising in the land or naval forces" to the narrowest limits consistent with the constitutional purpose of giving the Armed Forces disciplinary power over the troops. The contrary course would lead to a widening of the jurisdiction of the military with a consequent loss of liberty of the people.

The injury would not be the loss of jury trial alone. It might be the loss of other constitutional safeguards. For example, Article III, Section 3, defines the crime of treason and adds, "No person shall be convicted of treason unless on the testimony of two witnesses to the same overt act, or on confession in open court." If military tribunals could broaden their jurisdiction to try civilians who had committed treason, the important procedural safeguard contained in Article III, Section 3, would also be swept away.

Article 104 of the Code of Military Justice subjects to

court-martial "any person who (1) aids, or attempts to aid, the enemy with arms, ammunition, supplies, money, or other thing; or (2) without proper authority, knowingly harbors or protects or gives intelligence to, or communicates or corresponds with or holds any intercourse with the enemy, either directly or indirectly." This Article, in various wordings, has a long history, going back before our Constitution was adopted and re-enacted after it was ratified. For most of its history it has been phrased in language broad enough to include civilians. And it has been construed in military circles to be applicable to civilians in time of war. In 1863 it was, indeed, applied to William T. Smithson, a civilian, who was tried by court-martial for giving intelligence to the enemy by means of a letter, found guilty, and sentenced to five years. During the Civil War the military tried and convicted many civilians for this offense. See Winthrop, *Military Law and Precedents* (2d ed.), p. 103. The Judge Advocate General ruled that it was essential for the military to have jurisdiction over this offense:

"Without the authority to visit upon this class of offenses summary and severe punishments, the war making power would be greatly enfeebled if not absolutely paralyzed. Proceedings in the ordinary criminal courts, by indictment and jury trial would have no terror for such traitors through whose machinations indeed, the military power of the country might be overthrown, before the machinery of such courts could be even set in motion. To confine the exercise of this authority to those actually in the military service would be absolutely to defeat its object, since those who convey intelligence to the enemy, are not to be found among officers and soldiers who are offering up their lives for the government, but among demoralized and disloyal classes outside of the army. If such cannot be promptly and unsparingly punished, there can be no successful prosecution of hostilities."

The Judge Advocate thought the war power was sufficient to give the Congress the right to extend military jurisdiction over such civilians. He also ruled that a civilian transmitting intelligence to the enemy presented a case "arising in the land or naval forces" within the meaning of the Fifth Amendment, "since it directly connects itself with the operations and safety of these forces, whose overthrow and destruction it seeks."

That is, indeed, dangerous doctrine, for it allows the war power to override other express provisions of the Constitution. The citizen who gives information to the enemy certainly commits treason. And the provisions of Article III, Section 3, governing the trial of treason cases, are applicable in time of war. Referring to the Smithson case, Professor Edmund M. Morgan wrote, "Every act of treason would, by this reasoning, be punishable by court martial, and the third section of article III of the Constitution would have no field of operation." *Court-Martial Jurisdiction over Non-Military Persons under the Articles of War,* 4 Minn. L. Rev. 79, 106.

The same difficulty, so far as citizens are concerned, is

apparent when we turn to Article 106 of the Code of Military Justice: "Any person who in time of war is found lurking as a spy or acting as a spy in or about any place, vessel, or aircraft, within the control or jurisdiction of the armed forces of the United States, or in or about any shipyard, any manufacturing or industrial plant, or any other place or institution engaged in work in aid of the prosecution of the war by the United States, or elsewhere, shall be tried by a general court-martial or by a military commission and on conviction shall be punished by death."

This provision, which was extended to civilians in the Civil War, now has a scope so broad as to include almost any espionage done by a citizen. If it is valid, the provision of the Constitution defining and curtailing the law of treason becomes a virtual dead letter.

In World War I an attempt, described in Rankin, *When the Civil Law Fails*, pp. 138–139, was made to enact a law which would have punished spies by military trials, the theory being that the entire United States was in the war zone and that the establishment of martial law was necessary for winning the war. The bill died in committee after President Wilson announced against it. He said, "I think that it is not only unconstitutional, but that in character it would put us upon the level of the very people we are fighting and affecting to despise."

A citizen who joins the enemy forces and invades the country to operate as a saboteur commits more than an act of treason; he violates a recognized "law of war" as the Court held in *Ex parte Quirin*, 317 U.S. 1. But for acts which add up to no more than treason, he should be tried, not by the military, but by the civil courts, where he will receive the benefit of a jury trial and the special procedural safeguards erected around all trials for treason.

There can be no doubt that there is a small and limited group of civilians subject to military jurisdiction *in time of war*. Article 2(10) of the Code of Military Justice subjects to the jurisdiction of the military "In time of war, all persons serving with or accompanying an armed force in the field." This provision goes back to Article 32 of the Articles of War of June 30, 1775, which subjected to military authority "all sutlers and retainers to a camp, and all persons whatsoever, serving with the continental army in the field." As our leading authority on military law has written concerning this Article, "A civil offender who is not certainly within its terms cannot be subjected under it to a military trial in time of war with any more legality than he could be subjected to such a trial in time of peace." Winthrop, *Military Law and Precedents* (2d ed.), p. 100. According to Winthrop, this group "consisted mostly of civilian clerks, teamsters, laborers and other employees of the different staff departments, hospital officials, and attendants, veterinarians, interpreters, guides, scouts and spies, and men employed on transports and military railroads and as telegraph operators, etc." *Id.*, p. 99. The test is provided by the Fifth Amendment—whether the particular instance is a case "arising in the land or naval forces." For a civilian to be "in the land or naval forces" it would seem that he must have some obligation to further the military mission of the Armed Forces and hence be necessarily subject to military discipline. Certainly the group of civilians amenable to military jurisdiction *in time of war* is very narrow.

Efforts, however, have been made to enlarge the group by legislative fiat. Thus the Act of July 17, 1862, § 16, 12 Stat. 594, 596, provided:

"That whenever any contractor for subsistence, clothing, arms, ammunition, munitions of war, and for every description of supplies for the army or navy of the United States, shall be found guilty by a court-martial of fraud or wilful neglect of duty, he shall be punished by fine, imprisonment, or such other punishment as the court-martial shall adjudge; and any person who shall contract to furnish supplies of any kind or description for the army or navy *he* shall be deemed and taken as a part of the land or naval forces of the United States, for which he shall contract to furnish said supplies, and be subject to the rules and regulations for the government of the land and naval forces of the United States."

Under this statute a civilian who contracted with the Army to deliver supplies became subject to a court-martial. The reason for putting contractors under courts-martial was plainly stated in the debates in the House:

". . . A contractor who is satisfied that a prompt and certain punishment follows any perpetration of fraud will be deterred from any interference with the arrangements of the Army more certainly than if he could postpone the trial under the dilatory proceedings of the civil law. Hence the propriety of putting him under the

189

laws and articles of war. He interferes with the arrangements of the Army, hinders, obstructs, and weakens the military arm, and to that arm he may properly be made responsible." Cong. Globe, 37th Cong., 2d Sess., p. 2685.

It seems that the courts-martial were busy in the Civil War days trying civilians. Some were acquitted. Many were found guilty.

Daniel Wormer was found guilty by a court-martial for failure to deliver cavalry horses pursuant to a contract and was fined $2,000.

Sewall Buntnall was fined $1,000 for attempting to bribe a government inspector passing on wood delivered under a contract.

Benjamin C. Evans was fined $5,000 for failure to deliver clothing under a contract.

Augustus P. Dumont was fined $1,000 for failure to deliver clothing under a contract.

Samuel S. Smoot was fined $10,000 for failure to deliver cavalry horses under a contract.

John Spicer was fined $5,000 for failure to deliver cavalry horses under a contract.

E. Y. Beggs was fined $1,500 for failing to supply the quantity of wood he had contracted to furnish and for concealing the deficiency by artful and fraudulent piling.

Thomas D. Kidd was fined $1,000 for collecting money for manning, victualing, and running a transport, when the stipulated crew was not furnished.

Simon Silbernagel was fined $499.99 for supplying the Army with ulcerated and diseased meat, the light sentence being imposed "in consideration of the term of imprisonment already suffered by the prisoner."

William H. White was fined $3,000 for delivering rotten and inferior haversacks under a contract.

In these cases where fines were imposed the contractor was ordered imprisoned until the fine was paid, though usually a limit was put on the term of imprisonment—either one, two, or three years.

In other cases terms of imprisonment were imposed as part of the sentence.

J. C. Wilmore was fined $10,000 and imprisoned for two months for presenting false claims under a contract.

Charles Langenbein was fined $12,000 and imprisoned for a year for presenting false claims for the lodging and subsistence of army recruits.

Charles W. Hall was fined $10,000 and imprisoned six months for bribing army officers to pass horses tendered under a contract.

John K. Sletter was imprisoned for five years for delivering adulterated and impure coffee under a contract.

It was not until after the Civil War had ended that the judiciary caught up with this amazing procedure. In 1866 the case of *Ex parte Henderson* was decided by the Circuit Court for Kentucky, 11 Fed. Cas. 1067. Henderson was a contractor with the Army who was being held for trial before a court-martial. He petitioned for a writ of habeas corpus, challenging the jurisdiction of the Army to hold and try him. Judge Bland Ballard held that Congress had no power to provide for the trial of any person otherwise than by jury, "except in the exercise of their power to make rules and regulations for the government of the land and naval forces and of the militia in the service of the United States." *Id.*, p. 1076. Judge Ballard ruled that the performance by contractors under their government contracts did not fall within that exception. Though performance by the contractor is necessary for successful maintenance of the Army, so are many acts of civilians. If contractors could be tried by courts-martial, so could any private citizen "for failing or refusing to pay his taxes, or for discouraging volunteering, or for obstructing an enrollment or draft." *Id.*, p. 1077. "If the power of Congress is thus extensive, it certainly transcends every limit heretofore taught or imagined. Then have Congress power to convert the government into a military despotism, and to subject every man in the land to trial by military tribunals." *Id.*, p. 1077. Judge Ballard went on to say that Congress cannot "by mere enactment, place a man in the Army who is not." *Id.*, p. 1077. Accordingly he held that § 16 of the Act of July 17, 1862, was unconstitutional. The ruling was in the best tradition of the Bill of Rights.

In *Ex parte Weitz*, 256 F. 58, a civilian was held for court-martial when the automobile he was driving struck and killed a soldier within the limits of a military camp during World War I. The civilian was an automobile driver employed by a contractor who was doing construction work for the government at the camp. The automobile he was operating was owned by the contractor and was used for transporting civilians. The court held that he was not subject to military jurisdiction. This decision, too, is in the best tradition of the Bill of Rights.

When we turn to military trials of civilians *in time of peace,* quite different considerations come into play. There is no war to wage—no civilian is part of any military mission. These facts led Winthrop to write that in his opinion "a statute cannot be framed by which a civilian can lawfully be made amenable to the military jurisdiction in time of peace." *Military Law and Precedents* (2d ed.), p. 107. That was the prevailing view both in the Army and in the Navy. And it seems to me to be incontestable.

For a while the Articles of War subjected to military jurisdiction the inmates of the Old Soldiers Home in Washington, D. C. But this was too strong medicine even for the Army. The Judge Advocate General ruled that that law is "unconstitutional and a dead letter. These inmates are no part of the Army, nor are they supported by the United States. They are civilians occupying dwellings and sustained by funds held in trust for them." Op. J. A. G. 1912, p. 1010. The same ruling was made concerning a like provision of the law subjecting to military jurisdiction the inmates of the National Home for Disabled Volunteer Soldiers.

But the Army long maintained it had the right to try former officers and soldiers, who had been discharged and therefore had become civilians, for certain offenses committed by them while in the service. That provision is now contained in Article 3 of the Code of Military Justice.

In 1955, the Court held that provision unconstitutional. *Toth* v. *Quarles,* 350 U.S. 11. Toth had been honorably discharged from the Air Force after serving in Korea. A few months later he was arrested by the military for a murder said to have been committed while he was an airman in Korea. He challenged his confinement by a petition for a writ of habeas corpus. The Court ruled that the power of Congress to make rules for the government "of the land and naval forces," contained in Article I, Section 8 of the Constitution, restricted court-martial jurisdiction "to persons who are actually members or part of the armed forces." *Id.*, p. 15. All others are entitled to a jury trial and to all the procedural safeguards contained in the Fifth and Sixth Amendments.

The Court said:

"There are dangers lurking in military trials which were sought to be avoided by the Bill of Rights and Article III of our Constitution. Free countries of the world have tried to restrict military tribunals to the narrowest jurisdiction deemed absolutely essential to maintaining discipline among troops in active service. Even as late as the Seventeenth Century standing armies and courts-martial were not established institutions in England. Court-martial jurisdiction sprang from the belief that within the military ranks there is need for a prompt, ready-at-hand means of compelling obedience and order. But Army discipline will not be improved by court-martialing rather than trying by jury some civilian ex-soldier who has been wholly separated from the service for months, years or perhaps decades. Consequently considerations of discipline provide no excuse for new expansion of court-martial jurisdiction at the expense of the normal and constitutionally preferable system of trial by jury." *Id.*, pp. 22–23.

It was in this tradition that a New York court held in 1865 that a person arrested during the Civil War within the Union lines as a spy could not be tried by a military commission after the war ended. *In the Matter of Martin,* 45 Barb. 142.

In 1916 Congress extended court-martial jurisdiction *in time of peace* to still other classes of civilians. That provision was substantially the same as Article 2(11) of the present Code of Military Justice, which subjects to court-martial ". . . all persons serving with, employed by, or accompanying the armed forces without the continental limits of the United States. . . ." As in the case of the court-martial of army contractors during the Civil War, this provision was an attempt to expand the military jurisdiction that had been established over certain civilians *in time of war.* But the jurisdiction over civilians established by Article 2(11) is not limited to time of war. Yet when Congress subjected persons "accompanying" the Armed Forces outside the United States to trial by the military, it did so without any serious consideration of the constitutionality of the measure. The constitutional issues were, indeed, not presented to the courts until after World War II.

The first cases under Article 2(11) were decided by the Supreme Court in 1957.

Mrs. Clarice Covert was accused of killing her husband, an Air Force sergeant stationed in England. She was tried in England by a court-martial composed of Air Force officers. After her conviction was reversed by the Court of Military Appeals because of errors in the proceedings, she was held for retrial in the District of Columbia. Mrs. Covert petitioned for habeas corpus in the United States District Court, claiming that she could not be tried by the military.

Mrs. Dorothy Smith was accused of killing her Army officer husband while she was living with him at a post in Japan. She was tried by court-martial in Japan, found guilty, and sentenced to life imprisonment. While she was confined in a federal penitentiary, a petition for habeas corpus was filed on her behalf in a United States District Court.

The Supreme Court held that Congress had no power to subject either Mrs. Covert or Mrs. Smith to trial by court-martial. Mr. Justice Black said:

"The tradition of keeping the military subordinate to civilian authority may not be so strong in the minds of this generation as it was in the minds of those who wrote the Constitution. The idea that the relatives of soldiers could be denied a jury trial in a court of law and instead be tried by court-martial under the guise of regulating the armed forces would have seemed incredible to those men, in whose lifetime the right of the military to try *soldiers* for any offenses in time of peace had only been grudgingly conceded.

* * * *

"The exigencies which have required military rule on

the battle front are not present in areas where no conflict exists. Military trial of civilians 'in the field' is an extraordinary jurisdiction and it should not be expanded at the expense of the Bill of Rights. We agree with Colonel Winthrop, an expert on military jurisdiction, who declared: *'a statute cannot be framed by which a civilian can lawfully be made amenable to the military jurisdiction in time of peace.'*

* * * *

"Ours is a government of divided authority on the assumption that in division there is not only strength but freedom from tyranny. And under our Constitution courts of law alone are given power to try civilians for their offenses against the United States." *Reid* v. *Covert*, 354 U.S. 1, 23, 35, 40.

Extension of the jurisdiction of military tribunals over civilians, whether in time of peace or war, results in a diminution of the right of the people to be tried by juries in the civilian courts. That is a deep erosion of civil liberties. That is why the class of civilians amenable to military criminal justice must always be narrowly and closely defined.

IV. MARTIAL LAW

While there is mischief in the gradual expansion of the Articles of War into the civilian sector, there is greater mischief in the impact of the military on civil institutions during a war and in the days of uneasiness and fear that recur in peacetime.

In the early days of the Civil War, Lincoln, as Commander-in-Chief, issued an order: "That during the existing insurrection and as a necessary measure for suppressing the same, all rebels and insurgents, their aiders and abettors, within the United States, and all persons discouraging volunteer enlistments, resisting militia drafts, or guilty of any disloyal practice, affording aid and comfort to rebels against the authority of the United States, shall be subject to martial law, and liable to trial and punishment by courts-martial or military commissions."

Milligan, a civilian resident in Indiana, was arrested by the military, tried by a military commission, and sentenced to be hung. The charges against him were conspiring against the United States, affording aid and comfort to the enemy, inciting insurrection, and discouraging enlistments—all crimes defined by Congress and made punishable by the civil courts. Milligan, by a petition for a writ of habeas corpus, challenged the authority of the military commission to try him. The case reached the Court in 1866 and, in one of the most momentous decisions in its long history, it held that the trial of Milligan by a military commission was unconstitutional. *Ex parte Milligan*, 4 Wall. 2.

Though Indiana was, at the time of Milligan's arrest, in a theatre of military operations, the civil courts were open and functioning. It was held that so long as they were open, martial law could not be used to suspend the civil rights of citizens—an important one being the right to trial by jury. "Martial law," the Court said, "cannot arise from a threatened invasion. The necessity must be actual and present; the invasion real, such as effectually closes the courts and deposes the civil administration." *Id.*, p. 127. The Court went on to say that if there was a foreign invasion or civil war and the civil courts were actually closed and it was impossible to administer criminal justice according to law, the military could govern. "As necessity creates the rule, so it limits its duration; for if this government is continued after the courts are reinstated, it is a gross usurpation of power. Martial rule can never exist where the courts are open, and in the proper and unobstructed exercise of their jurisdiction." *Id.*, p. 127.

Those who conspired to take Lincoln's life were tried by a military commission and executed by its order. James Speed, the Attorney General in Lincoln's second Administration, maintained the legality of that action, even though the civil courts were open and functioning. But Edward Bates, Lincoln's first Attorney General, bitterly assailed the action, calling it illegal and unconstitutional. That has been the view of the scholars. It would seem clear that under the rule of *Ex parte Milligan*, such a trial could not be constitutionally justified.

The *Milligan* case has never been overruled. It stands as unimpeached authority for the view that, even in time of war, the right of the citizen to normal judicial procedure and to the guarantees of the Fifth and Sixth Amendments is secure, if he is outside the actual zone of warfare and if the administration of justice through the civil courts remains in fact unobstructed.

A regime of martial law may be lawful in time of peace as well as in war. As the Court stated in 1849 in the case of *Luther* v. *Borden,* 7 How. 1, 45, arising out of Dorr's Rebellion in Rhode Island, ". . . a State may use its military power to put down an armed insurrection, too strong to be controlled by the civil authority. The power is essential to the existence of every government, essential to the preservation of order and free institutions, and is as necessary to the States of this Union as to any other government."

Once martial law is established, the civil authority gives way to the military, at least to a degree. Searches and seizures may be made which would be beyond the authority of civilian officers. People may be killed in the actual clash of arms without liability. Suspects may be arrested. In other ways, as yet undefined, personal liberties may be impaired under martial law that would be denounced as outrageous violations of the Bill of Rights under a civilian regime. But Mr. Justice Roberts, writing in 1903, took the view that any action by the military beyond the bare necessities of law and order was illegal, absent an actual state of war. *The Case of Private Wadsworth,* 51 Amer. L. Reg. 63, 161. Under that view arrests might be justified, but not detention. Those arrested should be turned over to the civil authorities for trial and punishment. The power to detain a citizen at the whim of the military would indeed give the military the authority to suspend the writ of habeas corpus, as the Supreme Court of North Carolina noted in *Ex parte Moore*, 64 No. Car. 802, 807–808.

Certainly the military, operating to restore law and order under a regime of martial law, would have no authority to try and punish citizens. As a distinguished authority on this subject has written, "Martial law prevents, but it does not punish." Underhill, *Jurisdiction of Military Tribunals*, 12 Calif. L. Rev. 159, 178. If the insurrection or riot has closed the civil courts, it would be part of "the duty devolving upon the military" to open them, as the Supreme Court of Montana said in *In re McDonald*, 49 Mont. 454, 476.

There are expressions of opinion in some of the early cases that the authority to decide whether conditions are sufficiently acute to justify the establishment of martial law belongs exclusively to the President or the Governor, as the case may be, and that his decision is conclusive on all other persons. It was once stated by Justice Holmes, the libertarian, that the declaration of the Governor of Colorado that labor conditions in a certain county were so acute as to create a state of insurrection was "conclusive of that fact." *Moyer* v. *Peabody*, 212 U.S. 78, 83.

But it is now established that the final voice of authority in determining the lawfulness of military actions is the judiciary, not the military, nor the executive that authorizes the military to act, nor the legislative branch that sanctions martial law.

That was the view of Chief Justice Hughes, writing for a unanimous Court in *Sterling* v. *Constantin*, 287 U.S. 378. "What are the allowable limits of military discretion, and whether or not they have been overstepped in a particular case, are judicial questions." *Id.*, p. 401. In that case a federal court had set aside an order of the Railroad Commission of Texas which limited the production of oil from certain wells. The Governor declared martial law in the territory where these oil wells were located and ordered the state militia to limit the oil production as directed by the Railroad Commission. The lower federal court, in a suit to enjoin the Governor from pursuing that course, found that there had been no riot, tumult, or insurrection in Texas and that martial law had been illegally imposed. The Court sustained that finding, saying that "there was no military necessity which, from any point of view, could be taken to justify the action of the Governor in attempting to limit complainants' oil production, otherwise lawful. . . . There was no exigency which justified the Governor in attempting to enforce by executive or military order the restriction which the District Judge had restrained pending proper judicial inquiry." *Id.*, pp. 403–404.

The case is a minor one in the sweep of history. But there is no more important decision subjecting the military power to civilian authority. When the liberties of the citizens are involved, the judiciary has the final say on whether martial law is justified. Executive fiat is not enough. If the bounds of propriety are overstepped, the Executive and all those acting under him become trespassers. This is an important restraint in view of the whimsical and sometimes outrageous manner in which the power to declare "martial law" has been exercised by Governors of the States.

In 1913, after martial law had been declared to put down violence in a bitter mine strike in West Virginia, the Governor of West Virginia suppressed and closed the shop of a newspaper located outside the martial law zone for "aiding and abetting" the insurrection.

In 1920, after martial law was declared in Galveston by the Governor of Texas when a longshoreman's strike erupted into violence, a citizen was arrested by troops and fined by a military court for violating a traffic ordinance.

In 1933, the Governor of Oklahoma attempted to prevent Negroes from moving into white neighborhoods in Oklahoma City by declaring martial law and, in violation of the Fourteenth Amendment, establishing zones for white and colored people.

In 1935, after a political dispute, the Governor of South Carolina called out the militia to take charge of the offices of the State's highway commissioners, whom he accused of malfeasance in office. The troops set up machine guns and sentries in front of the commission offices.

In 1938 the Governor of Iowa declared martial law in an attempt to drive out an examiner of the National Labor Relations Board investigating a labor dispute in Iowa.

In 1938 the Governor of Tennessee, on the occasion of a primary election, called out the National Guard in Shelby County to intimidate antagonistic voters.

In 1939 the Governor of Georgia called out the National Guard to bar the chairman of the State's highway board from his offices after a state court had enjoined the Governor from removing him from office.

"Martial law" is a loose, vague term that has different meanings to different people. I put to one side the case where a military government is imposed on a conquered country. I speak of "martial law" only as it has been imposed on a part of our own domain; and I include those instances where without any declaration of martial law, the President has sent troops into a state to perform a mission on behalf of the federal government.

One of the most extravagant applications was in Hawaii during World War II. Immediately following the attack on Pearl Harbor, the Governor of Hawaii undertook by proclamation to place the Territory under "martial law." He was authorized by the Organic Act to take this action "in case of rebellion or invasion, or imminent danger thereof, when the public safety requires it." But his action in that regard was to remain in effect only until the President could act. The President approved the Governor's action on December 9. The regime which the Governor brought into being was a severe one. The Commanding General was authorized to exercise all the powers normally exercised by the Governor and by the judicial officers and employees of Hawaii. Pursuant to this authority the Commanding General established military courts to take the place of civil courts; and he forbade civil courts to summon jurors or witnesses or to try cases. A military government was installed in Hawaii with the Army exercising all legislative, executive, and judicial control. The grim story of what happened is recorded in Anthony, *Hawaii Under Army Rule* (1955). When the writ of habeas corpus was restored in 1943, there were many unseemly contests between the courts and the Army. *Id.*, pp. 64–77. The Army even undertook to prohibit judges from entertaining habeas corpus petitions. Thousands were convicted in these military courts and received sentences not authorized by the law of the land. Traffic violators got up to five years in prison; bail was abolished; and some were required to purchase war bonds or donate blood as part of the penalty for violating the law of the military. *Id.*, p. 106.

What happened in Hawaii was not the work of venal men filled with ambitions. They were honorable people, bent on defending their country. But the Hawaiian experience is a precedent to avoid. It proves, I think, that the military should be entrusted only with strictly military tasks, that all processes of government should be left in civilian hands, even in the darkest hour.

One reason is the nature of martial law as contrasted to civil administration.

Martial law in time of peace is a regime to put down riots, rebellion, and insurrection. Martial law in time of war is a regime to help wage the war successfully. Martial law, however invoked, is the use of force rather than persuasion, the rule by military edict rather than by laws made by representatives of the people, the assertion of arbitrary power rather than the due process of law guaranteed by the Constitution. Martial law and civil liberty are, therefore, in conflict. "The antagonism is irreconcilable," as *Ex parte Milligan*, 4 Wall. 1, 125, emphasized. That is the reason why the martial law that is allowable must be narrowly confined to the exigencies that make its invocation necessary.

The fact that it is necessary to call out the militia to quell a riot does not necessarily mean that the military have to take over all the functions of the police. The fact that some men need be arrested does not mean that the writ of habeas corpus need be suspended. The fact that manpower must be mobilized to meet impending invasion does not mean that the courts need be closed. The fact that hostilities are imminent does not mean that newspapers must submit to censorship. The fact that saboteurs may be at large who can be tried by the military does not mean that the military should also try traffic violations, domestic relation disputes, automobile accident cases, and ordinary criminal cases.

Moreover, the fact that troops must be called out to suppress insurrections or to enforce a court decree or to guard against invasion does not mean that a single function of the civil authorities must be disturbed. The American tradition has been just the reverse. In the Whisky Rebellion of 1794, Washington instructed the commander of the troops to see to it that the laws were enforced and to turn over any insurgents to the civil courts for trial. The objects of the military force were stated to be twofold:

1. "To overcome any armed opposition which may exist.

2. "To countenance and support the civil officers in the means of executing the laws." *Federal Aid in Domestic Disturbances*. S. Doc. No. 263, 67th Cong., 2d Sess., p. 31.

The instances where the President has sent federal troops into the States to perform various missions have been numerous. See Rich, *The Presidents and Civil Disorder* (1941). The purpose usually has been to protect federal property or to enforce a federal court decree or other law when it was felt that local enforcement machinery had broken down. In general, these were instances where military power was invoked to support, rather than to displace, the civilian authority.

It was in that tradition that the Court spoke in *Duncan* v. *Kahanamoku*, 327 U.S. 304, when it held that "martial law" as used in the Hawaiian Organic Act did not authorize a complete military government to be imposed on the people of the Islands even in time of war. "Martial law," while authorizing "the military to act vigorously for the maintenance of an orderly civil government and for the defense of the Islands against actual or threatened rebellion or invasion, was not intended to authorize the supplanting of courts by military tribunals." *Id.*, p. 324. In that case one petitioner had been convicted by a military court of embezzlement, the other for assault on two armed Marine sentries. The law under which the cases were tried was the law as it was made by the military. They wrote the law as they wanted it and attached such penalties as they desired. This was the regime of the garrison state—the very antithesis of a government of the people, by the people, and for the people.

The indictment which Andrew Johnson, in a famous veto message dated February 19, 1866, made of the military regime that Congress fastened on the South at the end of the Civil War can be repeated as respects Hawaii during World War II:

"The trials having their origin under this bill are to take place without the intervention of a jury and without any fixed rules of law or evidence. The rules on which offenses are to be 'heard and determined' by the numerous agents are such rules and regulations as the President, through the War Department, shall prescribe. No previous presentment is required nor any indictment charging the commission of a crime against the laws; but the trial must proceed on charges and specifications. The punishment will be, not what the law declares, but such as a court-martial may think proper; and from these arbitrary tribunals there lies no appeal, no writ of error to any of the courts in which the Constitution of the United States vests exclusively the judicial power of the country. . . .

"I can not reconcile a system of military jurisdiction of this kind with the words of the Constitution which declare that 'no person shall be held to answer for a capital or otherwise infamous crime unless on a presentment or indictment of a grand jury, except in cases arising in the land or naval forces, or in the militia when in actual service in time of war or public danger,' and that 'in all criminal prosecutions the accused shall enjoy the right to a speedy public trial by an impartial jury of the State and district wherein the crime shall have been committed.' The safeguards which the experience and wisdom of ages taught our fathers to establish as securities for the protection of the innocent, the punishment of the guilty, and the equal administration of justice are to be set aside, and for the sake of a more vigorous interposition in behalf of justice we are to take the risks of many acts of injustice that would necessarily follow from an almost countless number of agents established in every parish or county in nearly a third of the States of the Union, over whose decisions there is to be no supervision or control by the Federal courts. The power that would be thus placed in the hands of the President is such as in time of peace certainly ought never to be intrusted to any one man."

In periods of war Congress has at times provided that whoever violates a military order shall be guilty of an offense triable in the civil courts. Such was the Act of March 21, 1942, attaching a criminal penalty to violations of military orders concerning the evacuation of all persons of Japanese ancestry from West Coast areas during World War II. This was not an inauguration of a regime of martial law over the area. Congress and the President united in leaving to the military the decision as to the precise orders necessary to protect the West Coast areas from espionage and sabotage. But when the military decided that a certain course should be followed, the civilian authorities enforced it. The military determined that persons of Japanese ancestry—whether or not citizens—were great risks so far as espionage and sabotage were concerned. Accordingly curfew regulations and orders requiring the evacuation from the West Coast of persons of Japanese ancestry, whether citizens or aliens, were promulgated by the military. Citizens of Japanese ancestry who violated them were convicted and their convictions were sustained by the Supreme Court. *Hirabayashi* v. *United States,* 320 U.S. 81, involved the curfew order and *Korematsu* v. *United States,* 323 U.S. 214, the evacuation order. The question for the Court was not whether the orders were wise or prudent or necessary. That was a military decision. The judicial question was whether there was a "rational basis" for the decision of the military that persons of Japanese ancestry— some of whom were known to be disloyal—created a risk of espionage and sabotage and that time was so short that they could be dealt with only as a group, not on an individual basis.

While the Court sustained the convictions, the precedents established did not make the judiciary a rubber stamp for the military. They gave the judiciary final say as to whether deprivation of liberty of a citizen in time of war is constitutional. And when it came to the problem of detaining the Japanese after they had been evacuated from the West Coast, the Court held there was no such authority as respects persons who were loyal to the United States and against whom no charges had been preferred. *Ex parte Endo,* 323 U.S. 283. The Court said, "A citizen who is concededly loyal presents no problem of espionage or sabotage. Loyalty is a matter of the heart and mind, not of race, creed, or color. He who is loyal is by definition not a spy or a saboteur. When the power to detain is derived from the power to protect the war effort against espionage and sabotage, detention which has no relationship to that objective is unauthorized." *Id.*, p. 302.

V. CONCLUSION

It is a great and dangerous weakness to take the attitude that the military can solve our important problems. Yet that is a growing trend in the nation.

Max Radin said, "There is a strong tendency in time of war for many sober citizens to demand a severer, harsher, more drastic and more expeditious enforcement of all types of police regulations than they would endure in time of peace." This is a tendency that exists even in days of peace when world tensions keep the people in a continuous state of alarm or uneasiness. Hamilton stated the idea forcefully in No. VIII of the *Federalist:*

"Safety from external danger is the most powerful director of national conduct. Even the ardent love of liberty will, after a time, give way to its dictates. The violent destruction of life and property incident to war, the continual effort and alarm attendant on a state of continual danger, will compel nations the most attached to liberty to resort for repose and security to institutions which have a tendency to destroy their civil and political rights. To be more safe, they at length become willing to run the risk of being less free."

Today we are in a dangerous drift. Since World War II the military has been more and more in the ascendancy, as Professor Mills dramatically relates in *The Power Elite* (1956). I refer to the military bureaucracy, not to officers such as General Eisenhower who entered politics and received a mandate from the people. The great proportion of the federal budget spent on military matters—more than two dollars out of three—has helped catapult the military into a strategic position. Their planning is so vast and so secret as often to be beyond the reach of Congress. Yet, at the same time, they are now closely aligned with big business and occupy a commanding position over our internal affairs. The military has been given a more and more influential voice in determining our foreign policy.

These are political, not military decisions. The number of divisions in NATO, the existence of the Baghdad Pact, peace in Korea, the drawing of the line between South and North Vietnam at the 17th parallel, the retention of Formosa as a base—all of these involve military considerations. Yet each is a policy decision with large political implications. They are decisions which require a profound insight into the aspirations, motivations, and reactions of human beings at home and abroad. Yet more and more do the military dominate the making of such policies. More and more do the civilian agencies defer to their wishes.

In 1955 our military were so bold as to try to depose the progressive Ngo Dinh Diem as President of Vietnam and to restore Bao Dai, puppet emperor for the French. Only by the narrowest of margins was that political catastrophe averted. But it indicates the manner in which well-meaning military men, without understanding of political forces, surreptitiously intrude in affairs assigned by our Constitution to the civil authority.

A recent book by Masland and Rodway, entitled *Soldiers and Scholars: Military Education and National Policy* (1957), tells us what the educational requirements will be for the military if they are to qualify for high-level policy roles. A far more significant inquiry would be how to keep the military from meddling in civil affairs, how to keep the formulation of foreign policy out of the Pentagon, how to break up the alliance between big business and the Armed Forces, how to restore to the diplomats the problem of maintaining political equilibrium in the world.

The growing tendency in this country is to leave problems of civil defense to the Army. The danger of the trend —the idea that the military must take over the functions of civil government in time of war—has been clearly exposed by Fairman, *Government under Law in Time of Crisis* (1955). Yet the longing for security tends to develop confidence in a military regime. The idea "Let the Army do it" recurs with increasing frequency in days of tension and crises.

We need the force of public opinion marshaled against this trend. We need re-education in the fundamentals of democracy. The military mind specializes in military strategy, the training of members of the Armed Forces, their deployment in the field, and their maintenance and support. Those problems require a regime of centralized control and unswerving obedience.

The problems of civil administration are different. They

require leaders who know people, politics, and the art of persuasion, and who have the ability to organize a community on a voluntary, cooperative basis. The military operates in a chain of command. There is little individual initiative at the bottom. The civil administration is decentralized with units close to the grass roots of the nation. The military operates through orders that allow little or no deviation. The civil administration invites criticism; and through the functioning of a free press and free debate among subordinates, the civil administration is adaptable to easy change and modification. The civil administration operating on a voluntary basis elicits loyalties and devotion that no military edict can instill. The military regime has the appearance of efficiency. But actually it is in a strait jacket of orders that can only be obeyed, not debated. The civil administration is far more flexible.

The civil administration is the product of political processes rooted in the traditions of civil liberties and the rights of man. The military regime has a different expertise—that of war and combat. The civil administration brings to its task all of the great traditions embodied in the Bill of Rights. The military knows only short-cuts and substitutes.

Maintenance of civilian government in the event of an atomic attack will require the peacetime organization of an effective civilian agency capable of carrying on the functions of civilian defense under civilian control in time of emergency. Martial law would be the inevitable result of atomic war only if there were no arm of civilian government which was both prepared and able to assume the job of supplying leadership to the people and directing

214

the conduct of the essential functions of municipal government. Most of our state and local governments are not now fully equipped to handle this job in an emergency situation of the proportions of an all-out atomic war. And, although we now have a federal civil defense agency under civilian control and direction, its emergency powers under the Federal Civil Defense Act of 1951 do not permit it to direct the conduct of civilian affairs, even in the face of an atomic bombardment.

There is no good reason, even in time of war, why the military should gain any ascendancy over civil affairs. Civil courts can sit even while battle rages, unless the courthouse is in the battle lines. The FBI can ferret out saboteurs better than the military, for that is their profession. Prosecuting attorneys can bring malefactors to the bar of justice even while bombs fall. Civil agencies can be created in advance to care for the feeding, hospitalization, and the evacuation of bombed-out people. A national civilian agency can be empowered to direct and coördinate the municipal affairs of the country. There is, in truth, need to confine the military to strictly military tasks, leaving the burden of all other war problems to the civilian authorities. If that course is followed, civil rights will flourish in war as well as in peace. If we keep the civilian authority at all times supreme, we will not drift into the garrison state. We will find, I think, that government of the people, by the people, and for the people can flourish even in wartime, if the military are always subordinate. As Fairman has said, "For an ordeal of blood, sweat, and tears, a nation must draw upon its deepest spiritual roots. Army rule is not the sort of leadership that evokes an all-consuming popular effort—quite the contrary. The 'unspoken premise' that the Army must 'take over' is dangerous on spiritual as well as on administrative grounds."

There is wisdom in the tenet that the military should not take over the functions of civilian authorities even in days of war, unless the public danger makes it imperative. For as Briand said to Lloyd George in World War I, "War is much too serious a thing to be left to military men."

Index